NETWORKING
WITH WINDOWS 98

in eas

Peter Ingram

**COMPUTER
STEP**

In easy steps is an imprint of Computer Step
Southfield Road . Southam
Warwickshire CV47 OFB . England

Tel: 01926 817999 Fax: 01926 817005
http://www.computerstep.com

Reprinted 2000

Notice of Liability
Every effort has been made to ensure that this book contains accurate
and current information. However, Computer Step and the author shall
not be liable for any loss or damage suffered by readers as a result of
any information contained herein.

Trademarks
Microsoft® and Windows® are registered trademarks of Microsoft
Corporation. All other trademarks are acknowledged as belonging to
their respective companies.

Printed and bound in the United Kingdom

ISBN 1-84078-038-X

Contents

3   Network Interface Cards   47

4   Configuring Windows 98 for Networks   57

5   Managing the Network   73

Introducing Networks

Welcome to Networking in easy steps. The aim of this book is to allow a non-technical reader to build and configure a small network using Windows 98, and then be able to connect to the Internet.

This chapter provides a brief introduction to networks. We examine the basic concepts behind computer networking, and gain an understanding of Windows 98 networking capabilities.

We will take a brief non-technical look at the main networking protocols, and will also be looking at the relative merits of various types of network structures.

Covers

Chapter One

Why Network?

Have you ever found yourself rushing from one computer to another in your office or home, attending to several different jobs at various locations? Or do you often find yourself moving files that need printing from a PC that you happen to be working on to the PC that is connected to the printer?

You may have heard a lot about the advantages of using the Internet for sending e-mail, and decided that you want to get connected. Or perhaps you are already connected to the Internet through a single PC/Modem, but want all of your office colleagues to have access.

All of these situations can be made easier by allowing the various machines to communicate with each other – by networking the PCs.

This book will show you how to build a small network system using the inbuilt networking capabilities in Windows 98, and then how to connect this network to the Internet.

Networking Basics

Networking several computers together allows data to be transmitted from one machine to another in rapid and easily managed data streams. This sharing of data allows many of the resources that are located on a single machine to effectively become available to all other machines on the network.

These resources can be physically located on the machine (eg, as files on the hard disc), or connected logically to the machine. An example of a logically connected resource would be a printer that is connected to a PC, but which is then available over the network to other machines on that network.

An alternative situation would be where access to the Internet is available to all the PCs on a network through a special communication device attached to the network.

Access to all external and internal resources are thus made available to PC users on the network.

Networks allow users access to all available internal and external resources.

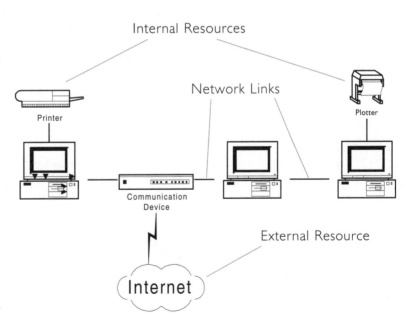

Networking with Windows 98

Windows 98 contains a number of integrated resources designed to enable communication between computers, both within a local network and between remote systems.

Network Protocols are control systems that control communication between computers.

This book will show you how to use these resources to build a small local area network (LAN), and to connect this network to the Internet.

Different types of networking systems use different digital languages to control the communication processes between computers. These languages are known as 'Network Protocols'. Windows 98 can be configured to accommodate many of the different types of networking protocols available. However, for the sake of simplicity and ease of installation, we will be using two of the most popular and widely supported protocols: the Ethernet protocol for the LAN, and the TCP/IP protocol for Internet access (the standard for global Internet communications).

TCP/IP is actually two protocols: TCP stands for Transmission Control Protocol and IP for Internet Protocol, the two being commonly combined.

Network Protocols

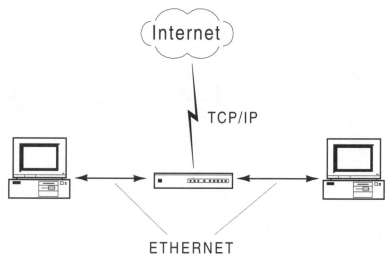

Resource Sharing

There are two main types of LAN system. The type used for larger networks is known as the Client/Server model. This model involves using a powerful computer that runs a Network Operating System and acts as the 'server'. The Network Operating System then runs and manages the network communication process from the server, supplying network services to the other 'client' computers.

These services might include the management of file transfers, running printing jobs, or even running applications across the network. For example, a word-processing software package running on a PC is actually being 'served' from the server across the network, rather than being loaded onto the PC's local hard disk.

The problem with the Client/Server model is that it requires specialised hardware, software, and to a large extent skilled networking technicians to configure and maintain the network. All of this can become expensive.

The second model, the Peer-to-Peer system or Resource Sharing, is fortunately a lot easier to implement and maintain, and it is this model that we will use in this book.

Resource Sharing is incorporated into Windows 98, and allows all network users access to all resources such as the hard drives, directories, printers, or CD-ROM drives that are available on the network. It also allows access to external resources across the network via special intermediary devices.

Resource Sharing involves each computer on the network taking an equal part in the networking process and is ideally suited to smaller networks.

Security

Being able to have complete access to all resources on the network is not always desirable. It is often the case that certain resources may need to be restricted to certain users.

Resources Sharing within Windows 98 allows for this, and incorporates the ability to protect access to particular resources with passwords. These passwords can then be stored within the Windows 98 configuration files so that access to protected resources is automatically assigned once the user has gained access to the network; the relevant password is therefore only entered once during the network login procedure. This function can also be disabled so that a password is required every single time the user attempts to access a protected resource.

Password access can also be configured to allow the user to read but not to change a particular resource, or to allow full access, including the ability to write to a resource (which would be necessary for sending jobs to a printer).

Each individual resource can also be configured separately so that different passwords and access rights can be assigned for different resources.

We will be covering all of these options in more detail when we come to configuring Windows 98 for networking.

What is Ethernet?

The Ethernet Protocol

Ethernet is the most popular protocol used for LAN communications. In essence it uses a digital 'packet' that can contain any other digital information.

Every computer that uses this protocol contains an ethernet Network Interface Card (NIC) that has a unique address code embedded into a microchip on the NIC. This address is used by the protocol to identify each individual computer. This allows every electronic packet that is sent from one machine to another to contain the destination address for which the packet is intended.

Every computer on the network 'listens' for packets that contain its own address. When a packet is placed on a network, that packet is broadcast to and received by every other computer on the network, but only the computer which corresponds to the destination address is allowed to claim that packet and receive the digital information contained within it.

Only a single packet is allowed onto the network at any one time, but the process operates at such a high speed that effectively the packet is delivered to the destination within milliseconds, allowing the next packet access to the network almost immediately.

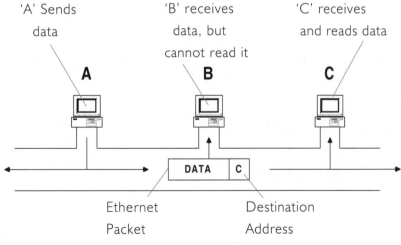

'A' Sends data

'B' receives data, but cannot read it

'C' receives and reads data

A   B   C

DATA C

Ethernet Packet

Destination Address

The Ethernet protocol also provides a means of preventing two computers from trying to place packets onto the network at the same time. When a NIC tries to place a packet onto the network, it first 'listens' to see if there is already a packet being transmitted to and from other machines. If so, then it is forced to wait for a random amount of time (milliseconds), before trying again. This continues until a 'gap' is found and then the packet can be successfully transmitted onto the network.

The Ethernet protocol provides a means of delivering data from any PC on the network to any other on the same network at a theoretical rate of up to 10 Mega bits per second. Ethernet can also be used to connect remotely located PCs, but this requires special communication links to be set up over specialised equipment.

Fast Ethernet

Fast Ethernet is a new standard of the ethernet protocol, based on the existing 10Mhz standard, but designed to operate at the much faster data rate of 100Mhz.

Mhz stands for megahertz or a million cycles per second and represents the operating frequency of the protocol.

The terms 'Mhz' and 'Mega bits per second' are often used interchangeably, but this is only true where one cycle represents one bit (a bit being a unit of data). For many protocols, this direct relationship holds true, but it is not always the case and so the terms should be used with caution.

What is TCP/IP?

The TCP/IP Protocol

As mentioned, TCP/IP is actually two protocols. These two protocols are almost invariably used together, hence the term TCP/IP has come to be accepted as describing a single system. We will be using this assumption here.

TCP/IP is the network protocol that is used throughout the Internet. It was originally developed in American academic institutions as a means of communicating between remote computers. It was the successful use of the TCP/IP protocol for communicating between university computer systems, first locally and then nationally across America and internationally between universities, that formed the basis of what is now known as the Internet.

It is the capability for being used over existing telephone systems that gives TCP/IP (and hence the Internet) its enormous potential for worldwide data communication. Ethernet is designed to run over relatively short distances at a very high data rate, but the physical limitations of the public phone systems mean that this high data rate cannot normally be sustained, except perhaps over the larger truck routes between countries and major cities. TCP/IP however is independent of the various data rates associated with different communication media, and so can be used over both very slow and very high speed systems.

Like Ethernet, the TCP/IP protocol uses an addressing system to determine the intended destination for a data packet, but unlike Ethernet, TCP/IP also includes a source address in the data packet. This system of addresses is used to route the data packet across the Internet, very much like the address on an envelope is used to route a letter across the various national postal systems. However, unlike Ethernet, each packet is not broadcast across the entire network, but is routed individually using the addressing system to a single destination. This system is known as 'packet switching'.

Packet Switching

When one computer communicates with another using the TCP/IP protocol, it breaks the information it needs to send into 'chunks' small enough for the TCP/IP packet to be able to handle, and then attaches a destination address and a source address. The packet is then sent out across the Internet, containing all of the information it needs to navigate its way to a remote destination.

It is a feature of the Internet that each individual packet can then take one of many different routes via the thousands of intermediate computer systems across the world to reach its final destination. Each computer along the way reads the destination address of the packet and routes it according to certain sets of rules to the next computer system on the Internet. This fragmenting of information and use of many alternative routes means that the receiving computer may well receive the packets in a different order to that in which they were sent. It must therefore have some means of making sure that it reads the incoming packets in the correct order.

The job of the 'TCP' part of TCP/IP is to ensure that each packet reaches its destination intact, and that the packets are numbered effectively so that the receiving computer can put the incoming packets back into the correct order. It is the 'IP' part of TCP/IP that looks after the addressing.

Because TCP/IP packets contain a source address as well as a destination address, the receiving computer system also has a way of replying automatically to the sender by simply reading the source address, and then generating another TCP/IP packet using this source address as the destination address for the new packet.

Another feature that is a very useful part of the TCP/IP protocol is that because each packet is essentially self-sufficient in its journey across the Internet, many packets from different sources can share a single communication channel, allowing perhaps hundreds of thousands of channels to share a single cable at the same time.

Network Topologies

The word 'topology' implies a description of how various elements within a system are related physically to each other. In the context of networking systems, we use several different ways of describing how computers might connect to each other via a cabling system. These different ways of connection relate to the different types of network protocol involved.

There are three main types of network topology, these being the Bus, Star, and Ring topologies. We will only be concerned here with the two that apply to the Ethernet protocol, these being the Bus and Star topologies.

Both of these cabling options will be covered later when we come to look at implementing a network cabling system. You, however, will need to make a decision about which is the most appropriate to your particular needs, based on the information contained here.

Bus Topology

The bus topology describes a system where each computer is linked to another by tapping into a common cable. The network system then shares a common single cable which runs from one computer to another. The network protocol must therefore contain some control system for gaining access to the network, so that several PCs are not using the same 'bus' at the same time.

The bus topology has one distinct advantage over other cabling systems. It uses a single cable and does not require additional hardware to implement the network. This makes this system relatively easy and inexpensive to implement.

However, there are several disadvantages in using this system. The main disadvantages concern system integrity. The bus must maintain continuity over its entire length in order to function. A single fault on the cable or its connectors can cause the whole system to generate errors or fail completely. The cable itself is rather prone to damage. A kink in the cable or excessive bending will cause errors on the network system.

This means that the cable must be well installed and protected at all times, as it represents the single most vulnerable element in the network. The necessity to maintain cable integrity also means that the connectors cannot be unplugged at the wallbox whilst the network is running.

Another disadvantage of using the bus topology concerns errors generated by the Network Interface Cards. Faulty NICs have a tendency to flood the network with a constant stream of nonsense data. This situation then effectively prevents other PCs from using the network. The Star topology is designed to eliminate this problem.

Finally, the bus topology currently only applies to 10MHz Ethernet. The faster 100MHz Ethernet will only operate over a suitable star configuration.

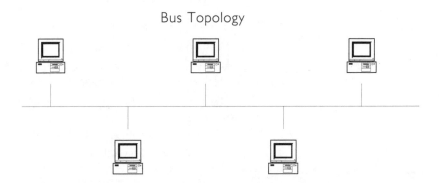

Bus Topology

Star Topology

The star topology describes a system where all computers are connected to a central distribution system. This central system usually involves a special piece of hardware dedicated to this function. This system allows for intelligent control systems to be incorporated into the distribution 'hub'. These intelligent control systems can be used for such functions as fault and error handling, system administration, and dynamic allocation of resources according to need.

The main disadvantages with this kind of topology relate to cost. As each PC requires its own cable, the costs of implementing a star system can be higher than those associated with, for example, the bus topology. The cost of a distribution hub must be taken into consideration.

One major advantage, however, apart from the functional considerations, is that the star topology has been adopted as the main international standard for data distribution cabling systems. This means that all future data distribution technologies will need to comply to this kind of topology, thereby protecting any investment.

Another more everyday advantage is that individual PCs can be disconnected at the wallbox outlets without affecting the rest of the network, as the hub simply detects the removal of the PC interface and reconfigures itself accordingly.

Star Topology

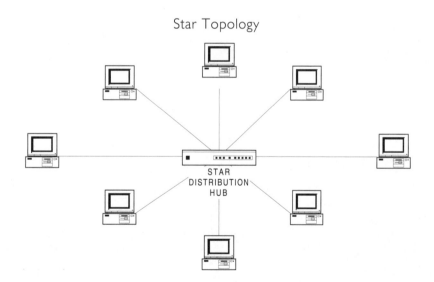

STAR
DISTRIBUTION
HUB

Ethernet Cabling Systems

The Ethernet protocol requires an operating frequency of 10Mhz. This represents a very high data rate, which requires special cabling systems in order to operate correctly.

Thinnet Ethernet uses the Bus topology and coax cable.

There are three main types of ethernet cabling system, but the earliest of these, known as the 'Thicknet' system, is now considered to be a little outdated and is definitely unsuitable for the small office environment, so we will not be considering this here.

The two types of Ethernet cabling system that we will look at are the 'Thinnet' system and the 'Twisted Pair' system.

Thinnet

Twisted Pair Ethernet uses the Star topology and twisted pair cable.

The first cabling systems used for Ethernet all involved using Coaxial (coax) cable. This is a special kind of cable where a centre copper core is surrounded by an air insulator which is then surrounded by a copper mesh, the whole arrangement being protected by a sheath. The coax cable was designed to overcome the problems associated with transmitting high data rates over normal copper-core cables.

Thinnet Ethernet uses the bus topology model to connect computers together. Thinnet is also known as the 10Base2 Ethernet system.

Twisted Pair

Twisting a pair of copper cables together in a controlled manufacturing process has been found to dramatically improve the data rate characteristics of ordinary copper cabling. When the Star topology was developed to overcome the problems associated with the Bus topology, this new kind of cable was used. Originally designed for 10MHz operation, this cable is now commonly available to 100MHz capabilities, and this has become the standard for most new data cable installations. Twisted Pair Ethernet is also known as 10BaseT or 100BaseT for Fast Ethernet.

Building the Network Cabling System

Having gained a basic understanding of the workings of a network and the types of network that we will be dealing with, we can now set about the process of building the network cabling system.

In this chapter, we will describe the types of cable that we may be using, and take a brief look at conduits and wall boxes. We will then look at designing and installing the two main types of cabling systems (ie, the Thinnet and the Twisted Pair).

Throughout this and subsequent chapters we will be referring to various items of hardware and tooling that will be required to build your network. Contact details of suggested vendors for these items can be found in the Useful Names and Addresses appendix (page 187).

Covers

Chapter Two

Types of Cabling

Thinnet

Thinnet uses a special kind of coax cable referred to by the coax cabling standards as type RG58 C/U. The main characteristics of this cable are an impedance rating of 50 Ohms, and an outside diameter of 4.95mm. Various cable manufacturers refer to this cable generically as Thinnet, Thin Ethernet or Cheapernet coax, and the specific characteristics may vary slightly from different vendors. Most will guarantee the cable to conform to the Ethernet standard, which is technically referred to as the IEEE 802.3 standard.

Twisted Pair (UTP)

The main international standards for copper data cabling systems are now based around the Twisted Pair model. This type of cable is available as two types, referred to as Category 3 (Cat3) UTP and Category 5 (Cat5) UTP, the 'UTP' standing for Unshielded Twisted Pair. Both types consist of eight copper cores arranged as four pairs twisted together and surrounded by a protective sheath. The twisting of the pairs is carefully controlled during the manufacturing process to give the high speed data carrying capacities associated with this kind of cable. The Cat 3 cable is rated to carry up to 10MHz, and the Cat 5 to 100MHz. As most new installations need to be 'future proofed' for new data technologies, the Cat 5 cable is generally the most popular, and as such is more widely available at little additional cost.

Twisted Pair (STP)

Twisted Pair cable is also available as 'shielded' Twisted Pair or STP. This type of cable contains an additional metal shield around the four pairs, and is used in installations where protection from excessive electrical noise is required (eg, in heavy engineering establishments). In most cases this type of additional protection is unnecessary.

Time to Decide!

Which of the two networking topologies you choose to implement will depend on your specific requirements and on the information in the previous chapter. Please skip whichever of the next sections describing the cable installations that does not apply to you. In later chapters we will deal with the choice of the different Network Interface Cards that connect your cabling system to the individual PCs, but with little difference in cost between these, we do not need to discuss the implications of this choice here.

Here is a quick recap of the advantages and disadvantages of the two cabling system types.

Thinnet 'ßus' System

Advantages:

• Inexpensive

Disadvantages:

• 10Mhz Ethernet only

• More vulnerable to network failure

Twisted Pair 'Star' System

Advantages:

• More compliant to International Standards

• 10 Mhz and 100Mhz Ethernet capability

• Less vulnerable to network failure

Disadvantages:

• Requires a distribution hub

• More cabling required

Conduits & Wall Boxes

If your working environment does not already contain an easily accessible cable ducting system, you may choose to use wall mounted conduits and wall boxes when installing your cabling system. It is well worth considering this, even though it will require extra expense and work, as this will protect your cabling system from damage. This is especially important for the Thinnet system. However, the multiple cables associated with the Twisted Pair system are also likely to require containment to prevent tangles of additional cables from cluttering up your working environment. It is worth noting here that both types of network topology can be accommodated by similar conduit systems, with just a few minor differences between the two.

Conduits

Plastic conduits with adhesive backings can be used, and these are available from most builders merchants, as either 16mm by 16mm, or 16mm by 25mm. The smaller is suitable for Thinnet installations and the larger for Twisted Pair. The larger dimensions may be necessary for the Twisted Pair arrangement as multiple cables may be routed through the conduits as opposed to the single cable need for the coax bus.

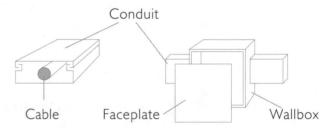

Conduit

Cable   Faceplate   Wallbox

Wall Boxes

The wall boxes consist of two parts: the backbox (which attaches to the wall) and the faceplate (which fits onto the front of the backbox). The backbox should be the standard 87mm by 87mm type used for many kinds of wall outlets. Thinnet installations should use backboxes that are 44mm deep, whereas the Twisted Pair connectors can be accommodated in backboxes 37mm deep.

...cont'd

Faceplates

The faceplates are of a specialised type depending on which type of network system is being installed. The specific type of faceplate required for each of the two network systems will be discussed in the relevant section.

Faceplates are available either as 'fixed' where the connector adapter is fixed directly into the faceplate, or 'modular', where the adapter is retained in a small mounting plate which then snaps into the faceplate. The modular arrangement allows different types of adapters to be combined at a single outlet (eg, to combine a network outlet module with a telephone outlet module).

Installation

Installing the conduit system is simply a matter of deciding the best routes for your cabling system, and then cutting your conduits to the appropriate lengths and fixing to the wall or to whatever surfaces are available. The conduits should be routed to your chosen wallbox locations, which are ideally positioned at about 30cm from the floor. If you have a raised floor or a ceiling void that is easily accessible, then you might consider laying your cables loose in these, and then routing your conduits directly up or down to the wallboxes, drilling suitable holes in the floor or ceiling.

In all cases, be careful to avoid running your data cabling parallel to any existing power or lighting cables within about 50cm. Crossing the paths of these existing power cables can be safely done provided the data cable crosses the power cable at right angles. Running active data cables in parallel to power cables can lead to induced currents, with a consequent degrading or failure of your network performance.

It is not recommended that you attach conduits to furniture, as it is likely that these will be moved at some point, thereby causing potential damage to the cabling system.

Thinnet Installation – Design

A coax network installation simply requires that the Thinnet coax cable runs from one PC to the next using the bus topology model.

The cable is typically installed in a conduit that runs around the walls of a room or office suite, with outlet wall points strategically located. At the outlets, the coax cable is routed out of a wall box to a PC and then back again to the wall box via the two wallbox adapter connectors on the wallbox faceplate. This arrangement maintains the bus topology.

It is technically feasible for the coax cabling to run loose from one PC to the next without the need for installing conduits or wall boxes. If you prefer to adopt this method, care must be taken not to damage or disturb the loose cables during the life of the network.

The coax cable connects to each PC via a specialised adapter called a 'T Piece' adapter which taps into the coax bus in a 'T' junction arrangement. This T junction arrangement is used at every PC, leaving the cable ends effectively loose at each end of the bus. These ends must be terminated using a specialised adapter which contains a 50 Ohm resistor. The termination adapters can either be fitted to the rear of the end faceplate adapters, or to the end T Pieces as shown.

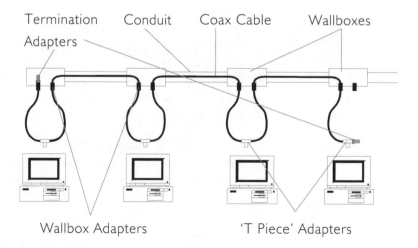

Termination Adapters   Conduit   Coax Cable   Wallboxes

Wallbox Adapters   'T Piece' Adapters

Distance Rules

The Thinnet system is defined by an Ethernet cabling standard that requires that certain distance and configuration rules are applied when designing and installing the cabling structure. These rules are as follows:

• A single coax bus is referred to as a segment. Each segment must not exceed 180 metres in length, including the combined lengths of all of the coax cables to and from the individual PCs.

• The distance between each T piece adapter on the bus must not be less than 0.5 metre.

• There must be no more than 30 PCs attached to a single segment.

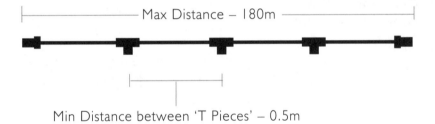

Max Distance – 180m

Min Distance between 'T Pieces' – 0.5m

Other Considerations

When designing and installing a coax cabling system, care must be taken to ensure that the cable does not bend excessively or kink at all. The ability of any coax cable to perform to its specifications will be severely affected by excessive bending and especially by kinking. A maximum bend radius is usually quoted for a particular type of coax cable, and for Thinnet cable this is usually about 20mm. That's about the bending you would get if you wrapped the cable around a jam jar!

Thinnet Installation – Cabling

Having designed the physical layout of your Thinnet system, and installed any conduits and wallboxes, you are now ready to install, terminate, and test the cabling.

What You Will Need

You will need the following before you begin:

Don't confuse the term 'Terminator', referring to the specialised adapter that fits onto the end of the coax bus, with the term 'termination', which is the procedure for fitting the Thinnet connectors to the coax cable.

- One Thinnet faceplate for each wallbox outlet. These will contain two Thinnet 'barrel' adapters.

- Thinnet coax cable sufficient to connect all of your PCs together in their planned physical locations. Allow approximately one metre of additional coax cable per wallbox outlet to allow an excess for the termination procedure. Don't forget to include enough cable for the 'flyleads' from the wallbox to the PC and back.

- Two Thinnet Terminator adapters; one for each end of the coax bus.

- One Thinnet T Piece adapter for each PC that you will be connecting to the network.

- Six Thinnet connectors for each PC on the network. That's four for connecting into and out of the Wallbox BNC adapters, and two for connecting to the T Piece adapter. If you are not using wallbox outlets then you will only need two Thinnet connectors for each PC, to connect to the T Piece adapter. Whichever way you decide to cable your system, it will probably be wise to purchase some spare Thinnet connectors, as mistakes during the termination procedure are quite likely before you get the hang of it!

- A BNC Crimp Tool, suitable for crimping the Thinnet connectors.

- A pair of cable cutters or pliers, for cutting the cable.

- A sharp knife, for cutting and trimming the coax sleeving.

- A small hand-held Multimeter, for testing the continuity and resistance of the finished cabling system.

As an alternative to the sharp knife, a Coax Wire Stripper tool is available that cuts the coax cable sleeving automatically in exactly the right places, and to the correct depth. If you are going to be doing many Thinnet terminations, then the slightly tricky setting up procedure for this tool may well be worth the effort!

Wrap some tape around the neck of the coax loop at the wallbox to prevent the cable being pulled back when laying the cable into the next wallbox.

Laying the Cable

Once you have acquired the necessary components for the cable installation, begin by laying the coax cable loosely into the conduits, allowing approximately 50cm of cable to loop out of the wallboxes. Once the cable is in the conduits, you can fit the conduit coverings as you will not need further access except for at the far ends of the cable bus, where the cable should be left loose inside the conduit ready to be terminated.

Terminating the Cable

The cable should now be terminated so that it will connect to the backs of the wallbox faceplate adapters.

First cut the loop as it emerges from the wallbox in the centre using the pliers, leaving two loose cable ends of approximately 25cm.

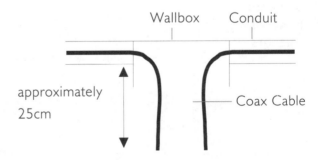

If you are using the automatic Coax Wire Stripper tool then prepare the cable ends according to the tooling instructions for RG58 coax cable type.

If you are not using the Coax Wire Stripper tool, then prepare the cable ends as follows:

1 Cut the cable back to allow enough length from the wallbox to enable you to manipulate the cable for termination, but not so long that the remaining cable length after termination will not fit comfortably inside the wallbox without excessive bending or kinking. This would normally be to about between 10–15cms from where the cable enters the wallbox from the conduit.

2 If you have been supplied with plastic or rubber cable support pieces, then thread this over the cable now. Then thread the crimp sleeve along the cable. Do this now as it may be difficult to thread it over after removing the outer cable sleeving.

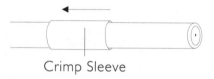

Crimp Sleeve

Square-off the end of the cable first, using the cable cutters.

3 Trim the outer jacket to 17mm from the end of the cable using the knife. Be careful not to damage the metal braiding directly underneath the outer sleeving. This can usually be accomplished by cutting lightly around the outer sleeving, and then by working the sleeving off, tearing the remaining plastic in the process.

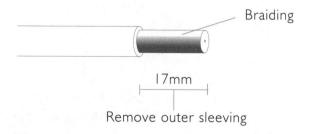

Braiding

17mm

Remove outer sleeving

4 Gently loosen the braiding so that it can be folded back over the cable, exposing the second plastic sleeving. You can ease this process by passing a sharp point forwards through the braiding to loosen the weave.

If there is a metal foil around the second plastic sleeving, then gently run a blade around the foil just forwards from where the braiding folds back, and remove.

Fold back braiding

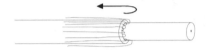

If you find that the cable sleeving slips for any reason during the trimming process, re-trim to the correct dimensions.

5 Trim the inner sleeving back to 5mm from the end of the cable, again taking care not to damage the copper core beneath. This will expose either a solid copper core, or a series of copper filaments, depending on the brand of cable that you have used. If you have copper filaments, twist them gently together. This a very important step as it will ensure that stray filaments are not left loose to cause a short circuit after inserting this section into the central pin.

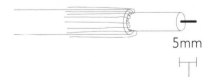

5mm

Remove inner sleeving

When crimping, lightly grip the pin or crimp sleeve within the appropriate indentation in the jaws of the crimp tool, and use this grip to ensure that the pin or crimp sleeve is fully butted before executing the crimp.

6 Insert the central core into the pin and crimp using the smaller indentations in the crimping tool. If you find that the twisted core will not fit into the pin, then gently untwist the filaments, carefully remove two or three filaments with the cable cutters, re-twist and insert back into the pin.

Crimp pin using crimp tool

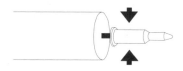

7 Push the connector body over the pin and cable assembly so that the pin produces a distinct 'click' as it locates correctly within the connector body. Try gently pulling the pin and cable assembly back out of the connector body. If you can do this easily then the pin has not located properly, possibly due to the core bending slightly behind the pin. If this is the case then re-insert and then firmly pull the pin from the front of the connector body using a pair of nose pliers, being careful not to damage the pin. You could use a piece of cloth between the pin and the jaws of the pliers to do this. Improper location of the pin is a common cause of poor network performance.

Push connector body
firmly to locate pin

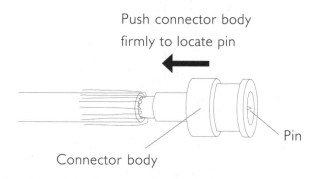

Connector body

Pin

8 Fold the braiding filaments back over the connector body so that they lie neatly and evenly around the outside of the knurled collar at the back of the connector body. If necessary, trim the filaments back so that they sit against the collar and end a few millimetres from the main connector body.

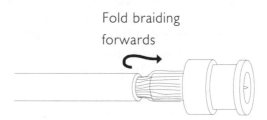

Fold braiding
forwards

9 Slide the crimp sleeve (the one that you put on the cable in Step 2) forwards and over the braiding until it butts against the back of the connector body. The braiding will now be trapped between the knurled collar and the crimp sleeve. Now crimp the crimp sleeve using the larger indentation on the crimp tool (ensure that the crimp sleeve stays butted against the back of the connector body during the crimp operation).

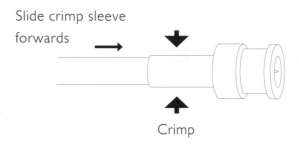

Slide crimp sleeve
forwards

Crimp

Any cable support can now be slid forwards over the crimp sleeve to complete the termination process.

Having completed the first termination, repeat the process for all of the wallbox rear connections, and for the far ends of the cable bus.

When all of the terminations are complete, add the Terminator Adapters to both ends of the cable, and plug in all of the terminated wallbox connectors into the rear of the Thinnet faceplates. Ensure that the connected faceplates will mount comfortably onto the wallboxes without undue bending or kinking of the coax cable behind the faceplates, but do not screw into place yet, leaving the faceplates loose for the time being.

Coax Flyleads

Now cut two lengths of coax cable for each PC, sufficient to reach from the wallbox to the back of the PC and allowing for any routing around furniture, etc. Remember that these cable lengths are the most vulnerable to potential damage from users, and route them so that the possibilities of damage are minimised. Do not, of course, run cables across walkways, etc, where they will present a 'trip' hazard.

Terminate both ends of all of these 'flyleads' using the same procedure as described above.

For each PC, connect both flyleads to the 'straight through' part of the T Piece adapter, and then connect the other ends of the flyleads into the Thinnet faceplate at the wallbox.

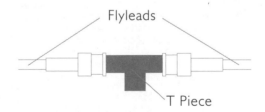

Flyleads

T Piece

You should now have a complete coax bus, with Thinnet Terminator adapters at each end, and the coax cable bus running in and out of the wallboxes from one T Piece adapter to the next.

...cont'd

Testing the Coax Bus

Testing the coax bus is a relatively simple matter of checking the electrical continuity of the bus circuit using a small Multimeter. This is best done by checking at the T Piece adapters for the combined electrical effect of the presence of both Terminator Adapters at either end of the coax bus. Any breaks or shorts in the circuit will then show up as an incorrect reading.

Firstly, ensure that your bus is complete, with all wallbox, T Piece, and Terminator adapter connections in place.

Set up your Multimeter to read up to 50 Ohms (refer to the Multimeter instructions if you are not sure how to do this). Then read the resistance between the exposed central pin and the connector body of any of the T Piece adapters on the bus.

If this reading is between 20 and 30 Ohms, then congratulations! – your coax bus cabling system is complete and functional. It should ideally read about 25 Ohms, this being the combined result of the two 50 Ohm resistors within the Terminator adapters, arranged 'in series'.

If not, then there is either a shorted or broken circuit somewhere along the length of the bus. If the resistance reading is close to zero Ohms, this indicates a short; if the reading is close to infinity, this would indicate a break in the circuit.

Test for the location of a fault as follows:

Start at left-hand end of the bus. Remove the Terminator adapter and, using the Multimeter set up as before, check for a reading of approximately 50 Ohms resistance between the central pin and the body of the Terminator adapter. If this is correct, then reconnect the Terminator adapter, and move to the first wallbox along the bus. Otherwise you will need to replace the Terminator adapter.

2 Disconnect the left-hand connector from the rear of the wallbox faceplate, and check the resistance across this connector. If the left-hand connector produces the correct reading, then this section of the bus so far is functional, and the problem must therefore lie further along the bus. If not, then the fault lies between the left-hand Terminator adapter and this connector. As the fault is unlikely to be within the cable itself, then one of the two connectors between here and the left-hand Terminator adapter is likely to be the cause of the fault. As there is no way to test exactly which of the two is causing the problem, you will need to re-terminate first one, and test, and then the other if this does not solve the problem.

3 Having established that the bus is functional to this point and that any further faults must lie further along the bus, reconnect the left-hand connector to the rear of the wallbox faceplate. Then disconnect the right-hand connector from the rear of the wallbox faceplate, and test both sides in the same way as before. If the reading to the left-hand side is now incorrect then the fault lies along the flylead section external to the faceplate. You can then isolate which particular section is responsible by testing to the left at the T Piece.

You can see that this is a process of moving along the bus to each wallbox in turn, then breaking the bus and testing backwards to check for continuity to the left-hand Terminator adapter at each point, correcting any errors that appear as you go. Continue this process until both sides of the bus produce the correct resistance, or until you reach the right-hand Terminator adapter. Finally, test this for 50 Ohms resistance. When you are satisfied that any faults have been corrected, reconnecting the entire bus will produce a combined resistance of 25 Ohms at the T Piece.

Twisted Pair Installation – Design

A twisted pair network is based around a central distribution hub. The function of the Ethernet hub is to receive incoming ethernet packets from a PC, and then to broadcast these unchanged to all other PCs on the network. The hub is often referred to as a repeater hub, because of the process of receiving ethernet packets and then relaying or 'repeating' them to several other PCs.

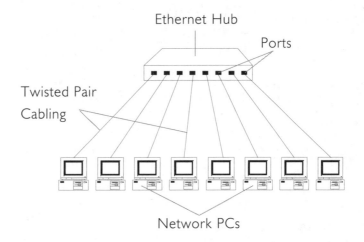

All of the network PCs are connected to the hub via individual twisted pair cables to ports on the hub device.

The main advantage of this arrangement is that a fault in any single cable or PC interface on the network can be detected at the hub, and automatically isolated from the rest of the network. This ability to 'intelligently' isolate faults is a common feature of most Ethernet hubs.

There are various types of Ethernet hubs available, and we will deal with these later (on page 46), but for the moment we will simply treat the hub as a device with several ports.

The cabling simply consists of running individual twisted pair cables from each PC to a port on the hub. This can either by done directly, or by running the cabling through a conduit system to strategically located wallboxes, and then via a 'flylead' to the PC.

The connection to both the PC interface and to the hub is via a standard connector commonly known as the RJ45 Modular plug.

The adapter socket used at the wallbox is similar to the one used at the ports on the hub, and is commonly known as an RJ45 Outlet Module, or a Cat 5 Outlet Module to denote compliance to the more modern 100Mhz standards.

In designing the twisted pair cabling system we will assume compliance to the Cat 5 standard, and Unshielded Twisted Pair (UTP) cabling.

Remember to observe the rules about running parallel to and across power lines (p25) when designing your cabling system layout.

Distance Rules

When designing a Twisted Pair cabling system, certain distance limitations must be considered. These limitations are due to electrical standards requirements that must be met when the ethernet hubs are designed, and simply state that the end-to-end distance between the hub and the PC interface must not exceed 100 metres. This is further modified to take account of the use of flyleads and wallbox interfaces, etc, such that in this instance the total length of the flylead must not exceed 5 metres, with the remaining 95 metres allowed for the main cable.

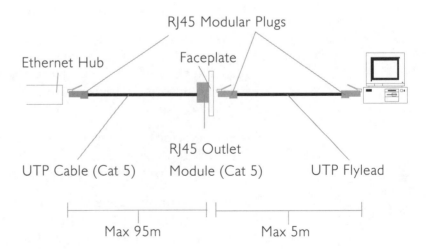

Twisted Pair Installation – Cabling

Having designed the physical layout of your Twisted Pair system, and installed any conduits and wallboxes, you are now ready to install, terminate, and test the cabling.

What You Will Need

You will need the following before you begin:

- One Cat 5 RJ45 faceplate for each wallbox outlet. These will contain one or two Cat 5 RJ45 Outlet Modules in either a fixed or modular arrangement (see 'Beware' on page 41).

- Two or three 'stuffer caps', for punching down the twisted pair cores at the punchdown blocks on the Outlet Modules.

- Cat 5 UTP cable sufficient to connect the hub to all of the PCs in their planned physical locations. Allow approximately 50cm of additional cable per RJ45 outlet to provide an excess for the termination procedure. Don't forget to include enough cable for the 'flylead' from the wallbox to the PC.

 An alternative to making your own flyleads is to purchase them ready-made. These are frequently more flexible as they use a different kind of UTP cable that is specially designed for this purpose. Always make sure that they are Cat 5 compliant.

- Three RJ45 Modular Plugs for each PC on the network. That's two for the flylead, and one for connecting to the Ethernet hub. If you are not using wallbox outlets then you will only need two RJ45 plugs to connect the hub directly to the PC. It will probably be wise to purchase some spare RJ45 Modular Plugs, as mistakes during the termination procedure are quite likely!

- An RJ45 Termination Tool.

- A pair of small cable cutters or pliers, for cutting the cable.

- A sharp knife, for cutting and trimming the UTP sleeving.

- A small hand-held Multimeter, for testing the continuity of the finished cabling system.

Twisted Pair Installation – Cabling...cont'd

Hub Location

The hub can be located in any convenient position that has access to a power point. It is common for the hub to be kept somewhere secure to avoid any accidental disconnection or tampering.

If the total span of the network exceeds 100 metres, then it would be sensible to locate the hub somewhere near the middle of the system to prevent the cabling distance rules being broken.

Laying the Cable

Tie a loose knot in the cable where it enters the wallbox to prevent the cable from pulling back.

Once you have acquired the necessary components for the cable installation, begin by laying the UTP cable loosely into the conduits. Allow approximately 25cm of cable to extend out of the wallboxes for termination, and enough cable to reach to the hub location at the other end. Once the cable is in the conduits, you can fit the conduit coverings as you should not need further access to the cable within.

Terminating the Cable

As you lay each cable between the hub and the wallbox outlet, mark the cable at both ends with a sequential numbering system using tape, or a marker pen. This will allow you to identify which cable goes to which wallbox.

The UTP cable contains 8 copper cores, arranged in four pairs, and colour coded according to an international standard. This colour coding is used to ensure correct termination at the RJ45 Modular Plug and at the rear of the RJ45 Outlet Module.

Terminating the Outlet Module

Terminating the UTP cable onto the Cat 5 Outlet Module is done by 'punching down' the cable cores into 'punchdown blocks' on the Outlet Module. Terminate the UTP cable (to the RJ45 Outlet Module) at the wallbox as follows:

1 Cut back the UTP cable to about 15cm from the point where it enters the wallbox cavity, using the cable cutters.

2 Trim the outer jacket to 50mm from the end of the cable using the knife. Be very careful not to damage the insulation of the individual cores directly underneath the outer sleeving.

...cont'd

There are many different types of RJ45 Outlet Module available, but all with identical functions. The main difference is that some require a specialised and relatively expensive 'punchdown' tool, while others supply some form of stuffer cap. I have shown one of the more popular Outlet Modules that uses stuffer caps (or you could use an Insertion Tool) but the basic termination principle will be the same for most types of RJ45 outlet.

This can usually be accomplished by cutting lightly to a depth of about 1mm around the outer sleeving, and then by working the sleeving off, tearing the remaining plastic in the process.

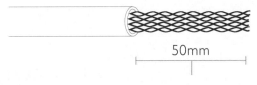

50mm

Remove outer sleeving

You will find that the cores are colour coded and arranged in pairs as follows:

*   Green/White & White/Green
*   Orange/White & White/Orange
*   Blue/White & White/Blue
*   Brown/White & White/Brown

You will also find that the 'punchdown block' on the Outlet Module is colour coded in a similar way.

3   Arrange the twisted pairs so that the green and brown pairs lie to the left, and the blue and orange pairs lie to the right at 90 degrees to the cable. The cable is then placed in the gap between the two punchdown blocks, so that the twisted pairs lie in the gap between the punchdown blocks and the front section of the module.

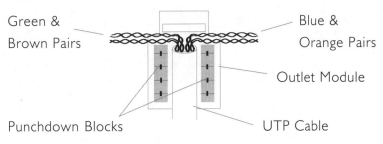

Green & Brown Pairs

Blue & Orange Pairs

Outlet Module

Punchdown Blocks

UTP Cable

Twisted Pair Installation – Cabling...cont'd

4 Untwist each pair a couple of turns, and guide each individual core into its respective slot according to the colour coding. Take care not to untwist the pairs by more than about 15mm from the termination slot. Untwisting a pair by more than this can affect network performance at high speeds.

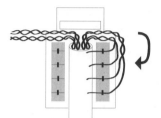

Guide cores into slots according to colour code

If you cannot obtain Stuffer Caps, then an 'Insertion Tool' (see Part Numbers – page 188) will serve the same purpose.

5 The stuffer cap is then pushed over the top of the punchdown block, and forced down until the cores appear at the limit of the slots in the stuffer cap. If you are feeling strong, placing the Outlet Module on a hard surface and pushing down firmly with the thumb should provide enough 'punchdown' force. Otherwise, tap lightly down with a tack hammer, or use a pair of slip pliers.

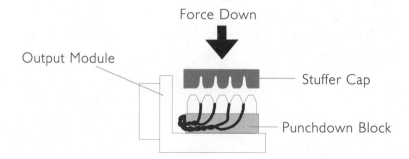

Force Down

Output Module

Stuffer Cap

Punchdown Block

6 Excess cores in the gap between the punchdown blocks can then be removed by carefully running a sharp blade along the inside ledge on the punchdown block, taking care not to damage the cable.

Terminating the Modular Plug

Terminating the UTP cable with an RJ45 Modular Plug requires the use of a specialised termination tool.

You will need to terminate the cables that will connect to the hub, as well as the flyleads that will connect the wallbox outlet to the PC. If you are using ready-made flyleads then the latter will not be necessary.

Terminate the Modular Plugs as follows:

1   If you have been provided with a Strain Relief boot for your plug, then feed this onto the cable first.

2   Trim the outer jacket to 20mm from the end of the cable using the knife. Be very careful not to damage the insulation of the individual cores directly underneath the outer sleeving.

20mm

Remove outer sleeving

3   Untwist the pairs and arrange the cores as shown.

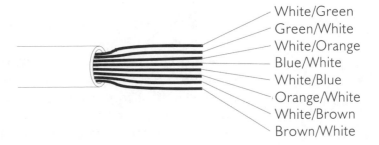

White/Green
Green/White
White/Orange
Blue/White
White/Blue
Orange/White
White/Brown
Brown/White

Arrange the cores so that they lie as flat as possible, and in as straight a line as possible, just as in the diagram above.

4 Use a sharp blade or the cable cutters to accurately trim the cores at a right angle to the cable, to 13mm from the cable sleeving.

13mm

Trim cores at right angle to cable.

5 Check the order of the colour coding. Then, hold the RJ45 Modular Plug in your right hand so that the metal contacts are facing towards you and the rear of the plug is to the left, and hold the cable in your left hand so that the White/Green core is at the top. (If you are left handed, reverse this.) Slide the cores into the rear of the Modular Plug. If the cores are all lying flat and straight, you should find that they are guided smoothly into their separate channels. Push the cores in firmly so that they butt fully against the end of the plug.

6 With the cable fully butted into the plug, insert the plug into the termination tool and crimp to complete the termination. You can then slide any strain relief components along the cable and onto the back of the plug.

Testing the Twisted Pair Cabling

In order to test the twisted pair cabling system, we need to check electrical continuity between the pins on the Modular Plugs at either end of the link between the hub and the PC. As these plugs are likely to be at some distance from each other, testing across the length of the link will be difficult with a normal hand held Multimeter. The solution to this problem is to make a simple 'loop back' plug.

...cont'd

This plug will be fitted into the Outlet Module, and will connect the appropriate pairs of connection links together at the Outlet Module. This link completes the circuit at the Outlet Module, allowing us to test for continuity across the appropriate contacts at the hub-end Modular Plug.

Make up the 'loop back' plug as follows:

1 Terminate a length of UTP cable with a Modular Plug as before, and then cut the cable at about 5cm from the back of the plug. You will find it easier to do it this way, rather than to try and terminate a short length.

2 Remove about 3cm of the cable sleeving from the end of the cable, being careful as before not to damage the core insulation underneath. Separate the twisted pairs.

3 Then, one at a time, untwist each pair, strip the insulation from the core to expose the copper, and then twist the bare copper cores firmly back together so that Green/White connects to White/Green and so on. Cover each exposed contact with some tape to prevent shorting.

With this loop back plug, you can then test each link one at a time by inserting the loop back plug into the Outlet Module and testing for continuity using the Multimeter across the contacts at the hub-end Modular Plug that corresponds to the outlet.

Using the standard numbering system where, with the cable down and the metal contacts on the Modular Plug facing you, the left end pin is No.1 and the right end pin is No.8, test for continuity across the following contacts:

- 1&2 – Green pair
- 3&6 – Orange pair
- 4&5 – Blue pair
- 7&8 – Brown pair

Ethernet Hubs

Ethernet TP Hubs

Ethernet hubs are available in a wide variety of formats. The types suitable for twisted pair ethernet operations are known as 10BaseT or 100BaseT hubs, depending on the Ethernet speed. The '10' or '100' refers to the operating frequency (10Mhz or 100Mhz); the 'Base' refers to baseband which is the type of signalling used; and the 'T' refers to twisted pair.

10BaseT hubs are available as either rack mounted (which are designed to fit standard networking equipment racks) or desktop (which are designed to sit freely on a desktop or shelf). Rack mounted hubs are mainly used in large scale networks, whereas desktop hubs are more suitable for the small office environment.

Desktop hubs contain either four or (more usually) eight ethernet ports.

The simplest eight port hubs are perfectly adequate for our needs.

Other features that you may find are hubs that are SNMP compatible or that integrate other types of ethernet ports for connection to other types of ethernet media (eg, Fibre optics). SNMP stands for Simple Network Management Protocol, an advanced system that allows for a standardised form of network management.

Stackable Hubs

One feature that is available for ethernet hubs and may be useful is the ability to stack hubs together. This allows for the number of ports available to the network to be increased by connecting further hubs to the existing hub in a 'stacking' arrangement. This facility therefore allows for easy expansion of the initial network configuration as the need arises.

Network Interface Cards

In this chapter, we will look at the various types of Network Interface Cards (NICs) and their installation and configuration. We will also look at the special case of NICs suitable for Laptop PCs.

Covers

Chapter Three

Types of Network Interface Card

There are many different types of Ethernet NIC available, but all basically provide the same function (ie, to provide a hardware interface between an Ethernet network and the PC).

The differences between NICs fall into two main areas, these being:

Type of Connection to the Network

We have looked at two types of connection to the Ethernet network (ie, Coax and Twisted Pair). NICs are available with either a Coax connection (BNC), a Twisted Pair connection (RJ45) or both. You should specify which type of network connection you require.

Type of PC Architecture

The evolution of PCs over the last few years has seen a constant development in the type of internal 'architecture' that is used within the PC. The main component of any PC is the 'mother board'. This contains the central element of the computer, the processor or CPU (Central Processing Unit). The CPU communicates with the various internal elements of the PC via a 'bus'. The 'bus' also allows the CPU to communicate with other external devices, for example with a NIC.

Along with improvements in CPU technology, new types of internal bus architecture have been developed. These include the following:

- ISA   – Industry Standard Architecture

- VLB   – Vesa Local Bus

- PCI   – Peripheral Component Interface

- PCMCIA   – Personal Computer Memory Card International Association

Other more specialised types of architecture are also available, but these tend to be less common or involve a closely defined relationship with a specific vendor.

The type of architecture that your PC contains will determine the type of NIC that you should use. Each type of architecture is associated with a different type of motherboard interface connector; these are known simply as 'slots'. You may need to consult your PC manual to find out which type of bus architecture your PC will support. You may also need to look inside your PC to see which of the available interface slots are vacant.

You will probably find that your PC will support several types of bus architecture: most will still support the original standard (ie, the ISA bus) as well as one or more of the more advanced types of bus architecture (eg, VLB or PCI). In order to get the best performance from your NIC, you should attempt to purchase the type of NIC that is compatible with the main type of architecture in your PC (eg, VLB or PCI for newer PCs).

PCMCIA NICs

The PCMCIA interface (also laughingly referred to as the 'People Can't Manage Computer Industry Acronyms' interface!) is a specialised type of PC interface that was developed mainly for the smaller scales of integration associated with Laptop PCs. If you are considering connecting a Laptop (or Notebook) PC to your network, you will need to check that your Laptop will support a PCMCIA interface, and obtain a PCMCIA style of NIC.

NIC Installation

Installing the NIC is a matter of removing the PC cover and inserting the NIC into an available slot on the motherboard. Proceed as follows:

1 Ensure that the PC is switched off and disconnected from the mains power supply, then remove the PC cover.

2 Once the cover is removed you will see a series of slots on the motherboard. Based on the type of NIC that you have purchased (see previous section) select an available slot that matches the NIC interface.

3 Remove the backplate from this slot by removing the screw at the top of the backplate. Do not lose this screw! (eg, by dropping it into the internal PC workings as you remove it).

The NIC may be vulnerable to static. Before handling the NIC, make sure that you have discharged any static electricity in your body. This can be done by touching the bare metal of plumbing or central heating pipes, which discharges any static to earth.

4 Insert the NIC into the slot. Once inserted, the plate that contains the external connectors on the NIC should sit flush against the PC backplate mounting panel. You should push the NIC firmly into the motherboard slot to ensure a good connection, but do not force it: if it does not appear to fit you have either selected a slot that does not match the NIC interface, or the alignment is incorrect.

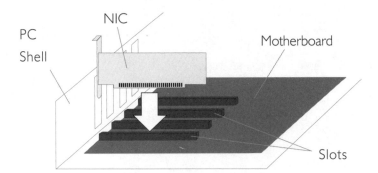

5 Secure the NIC with the backplate screw, replace the PC cover, and replace the mains cable.

NIC Configuration

In order for the NIC to function correctly under Windows 98, the correct hardware and driver software configurations will need to be implemented. This process is often an automated process, provided by a combination of the Windows 98 operating system and the manufacturer's installation software.

The precise procedure for configuring the NIC will depend to a large extent on your existing Windows 98 setup and the brand and type of NIC that you are using.

In general terms you should follow the manufacturers instructions. However, the following instructions may be useful as a guide in the event that any fully automated procedure does not go smoothly.

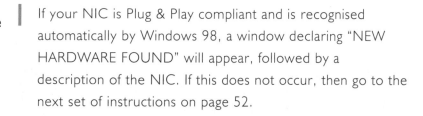 **If after restarting Windows 98 you are asked to enter a password, simply click 'OK' without entering a password.**

Before proceeding, you will need the original Windows 98 CD that you used to install your Windows 98 setup, and the NIC installation floppy provided with the NIC.

Having physically installed the NIC in the PC, switch on the PC and run Windows 98.

Automatic NIC Detection (Plug & Play)

If you have trouble locating a required file, try using the Windows 'Find' utility. This is available from 'Start > Find > Files or Folders'. You can search all available drives from here.

1 If your NIC is Plug & Play compliant and is recognised automatically by Windows 98, a window declaring "NEW HARDWARE FOUND" will appear, followed by a description of the NIC. If this does not occur, then go to the next set of instructions on page 52.

2 The necessary drivers will then be loaded automatically. You may be asked to insert the Windows 98 CD. If so, then do so and click 'OK'. If the CD is not located immediately (the CD drive can take a while to get up to speed) then wait for a few seconds before re-trying.

NIC Configuration...cont'd

3 Once the drivers have been loaded, the 'System Settings Change' window appears asking you to restart the computer. Click 'Yes'.

If the above procedure went smoothly, you can go straight to 'Checking the NIC Hardware Configuration' on page 54.

Non Automatic NIC Detection

If Windows 98 does not automatically recognise the NIC, then proceed as follows:

1 Click on the 'Start' button on the Windows 98 control bar, go to 'Settings' and click on 'Control Panel'.

2 On the Control Panel, double-click 'Add New Hardware'. This will start up the Add New Hardware Wizard. Click on 'Next>', and then on 'Next>' again in the rather spurious 'Windows will now search....etc' window. Windows will then conduct another search for Plug & Play devices.

3 When the 'Windows can now search for hardware that is not Plug & Play.....' window appears, select the 'No....' option and click 'Next>'.

4 Select the 'Network adapters' option from the list of hardware types (scroll down) and click on 'Next>'.

5 In the 'Select Devices' window that appears you are presented with a list of NIC manufacturers. If the manufacturer of your NIC is listed, select this item. A list of the different NIC models from that manufacturer which Windows 98 recognises is then presented in the right hand window. If your particular model of NIC is listed, then the drivers for this may be available from the Windows 98 CD. Select the appropriate model and click on 'OK'. If your model is not available continue with Step 6. Otherwise skip to Step 7.

If you find that the system cannot locate a file, then you can use the Windows 98 file finder to search all drives for the missing file. Click on 'Start', and then go to 'Find' and 'Files or Folders'.

6 If the drivers required for your NIC are not available from the Windows 98 CD you will need to install the drivers from the installation floppy disc or CD that was supplied by the manufacturer. From within the 'Select Devices' window, click on 'Have Disk'. You will then be prompted to insert the floppy disk into the A:\ drive. If installing from a CD, click on 'Browse' and select the CD drive. Once the manufacturers installation disk is in place, click 'OK'. From the 'Select Devices' window, select the model of NIC that you have and click on 'OK'. The appropriate files will then start to load.

7 Windows will automatically detect the hardware settings for the NIC and present the results. Click on 'Next>' to accept these settings. Windows will then attempt to install the necessary drivers (insert the Windows 98 CD when prompted to do so). After all of the necessary drivers have been installed the message 'Windows has finished installing the software......' will appear. Click on 'Finish' and then select 'Yes' to shut down the computer.

8 Restart the computer. If the 'Enter Network Password' window appears, click on 'OK' without entering a password.

Disabling Network Password

To disable the Network Password dialogue, proceed as follows:

1 In the Control Panel, double-click 'Network'. In the 'Network' window that appears you will see a section for setting the 'Primary Network Logon'. Make sure this is set to 'Windows Logon' from the drop-down selection list, then click 'OK'.

2 Click 'Yes' to restart the computer when the 'System Setting Change' window appears. When the system restarts the Network Password function is disabled .

Checking the NIC Hardware Configuration

The hardware driver for the NIC should now be installed. We now need to check that the setup does not conflict with other devices on the computer.

1 Start up the Control Panel as before. Double-click 'System', then select the 'Device Manager' tab.

2 Double-click 'Network adapters'. A description of your NIC should then appear – double-click this.

3 Under the 'General' tab, you will see a box entitled 'Device status'. If this states that 'This device is working properly', then there are no problems. If so, click 'OK', and then 'OK' again in the System Properties window to return to the Control Panel. Otherwise, proceed to the next section.

Resolving Hardware Conflicts

If you have identified a hardware conflict with your NIC setup, click the 'Resources' tab in the window describing the NIC device setup. You will see a window looking something like this, showing a 'Conflicting device list:'

1 Select conflicting item.

2 De-select 'Use automatic settings'.

3 Click 'Change Settings'.

4 Scroll through available settings until 'No devices are conflicting' shows.

5 Click on 'OK'.

6 Repeat this process for 'Input/Output Range'.

7 Click 'OK', and then 'Yes' to the question 'Do you want to continue?'.

8 Close the 'System Properties' Windows 98, and answer 'Yes' to the question 'Do you want to restart your computer now?'.

Laptop NIC Installation

Laptops use a specialised type of interface to allow access to external devices: the PCMCIA interface. This interface accepts miniaturised PCMCIA cards which can perform a wide range of functions eg. Fax/Modem, Network Interface, and storage devices. In order to install any of these devices into the laptop it is first necessary to configure Windows 98 for PCMCIA operation as follows:

1 Click on the 'Start' button on the Windows 98 control bar, go to 'Settings' and 'Control Panel'.

2 Double-click 'Add New Hardware' to start up the Add New Hardware Wizard. Click on 'Next>'and then 'Next>' again. If the 'Is the device that you want to install listed below' window appears, then select 'No' and click on 'Next>'. Otherwise, or following this, select 'No, I want to select...' and click 'Next>'.

3 Select 'PCMCIA Socket' (scroll down), and click 'Next>'.

4 A list of available manufacturers is displayed. If your make of laptop is listed, then select that option. You may then need to consult your laptop manual for instructions on installing the appropriate driver software. Otherwise, leave the selection on the 'Standard PCMCIA Drivers' and click 'Next>'.

5 The wizard will automatically select the appropriate hardware settings and display them. Click 'Next>'. Insert the Windows 98 CD if prompted. You will get a message telling you that 'The Windows drivers for your PC Card device are now installed'. Click 'Finish'.

You can now insert your NIC into the PCMCIA slot and configure the NIC as for PC installation (page 51).

Configuring Windows 98 for Networks

In this chapter, we will look at configuring the Windows 98 system for networking. We will also examine the Windows 98 file and printer sharing capabilities and the share level security system. Finally, we will look at the network monitoring and management utilities that are available under Windows 98.

Covers

Chapter Four

Installing Microsoft Network Client

Information on configuring Windows 98 for networks can be found by installing the Windows 98 Resource Kit files. To do this, run \tools\reskit\setup.exe **from the Windows 98 CD.**

In order for the PCs to communicate with each other across the network, it is necessary to install the Client for Microsoft Networks within the Windows 98 networking setup. To do this, proceed as follows:

1 Click on 'Start', then go to 'Settings' and 'Control Panel' and click. From the Control Panel, double-click on 'Network'.

2 A window similar to the following will appear. The list of installed networking components that appears in your window may well be different, but it should certainly include the NIC adapter driver that we installed in the previous chapter.

3 Check the list for an entry 'Client for Microsoft Networks'.

4 If not present, click 'Add'.

5 From the window that appears, double-click 'Client'.

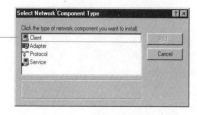

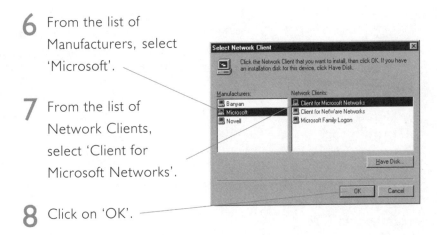

6 From the list of
Manufacturers, select
'Microsoft'.

7 From the list of
Network Clients,
select 'Client for
Microsoft Networks'.

8 Click on 'OK'.

The 'Client for Microsoft
Networks' will have been
added to the list.

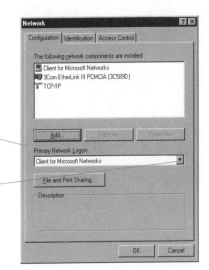

9 If the Primary
Network Logon has
changed to 'Client for
Microsoft Networks',
click on the drop
down selector and
click on 'Windows
Logon'.

You can now either click 'OK', which will prompt you to
restart Windows 98, or you can proceed directly to the next
section, ignoring the first instruction.

Installing Protocol Drivers

Having installed the client software for Windows 98 networking, we can now install the necessary protocol drivers. Windows 98 supports a wide variety of network protocols, but for our purposes we only need to install two.

The protocol that is required for immediate communication between PCs on the network is the NetBEUI protocol. Windows 98 also supports other protocols for this purpose, but in preference we will use the NetBEUI protocol as this is specifically designed for Windows 98 network communications.

You will notice that the TCP/IP protocol was installed automatically along with the Client for Microsoft Networks. This will allow our network to communicate with external TCP/IP systems such as the Internet.

To install the NetBEUI driver, proceed as follows:

| Open the Control Panel, and double-click 'Network' as before to open the Network configuration window.

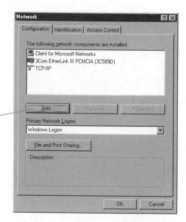

2 Click 'Add'.

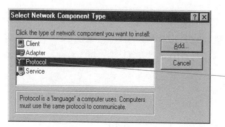

3 Select and double-click 'Protocol'.

4 Select 'Microsoft' from the list of Manufacturers.

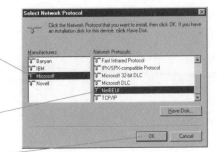

5 Select 'NetBEUI' from the list of Network Protocols.

6 Click 'OK'.

You may be required to insert the Windows 98 CD disk into the relevant drive.

If the TCP/IP is not installed, install it now by repeating the above procedure from Item 2 to Item 6, replacing Item 5 with the selection of the 'TCP/IP' protocol. We will be needing the TCP/IP driver later when we come to look at connecting to the Internet.

Once again, after installing the protocol drivers you can either click 'OK', and be prompted to restart Windows 98, or you can proceed directly to the next section. This will also apply to the next section, until all network configurations are complete.

It is worth pointing out here that if you are not using any other networking systems (eg, Novell Netware), that you can safely remove the IPX/SPX protocol if present simply by selecting it from the list and clicking the 'Remove' button. The same applies to the 'Client for Netware Networks' if listed.

Configuring Names and Workgroups

When Windows 98 was first installed on your computer(s), the installation asked for certain identification parameters to be specified. These included names for the user, the computer, and for workgroups. After the initial installation these names are then available to various advanced Windows 98 utilities for defining and customising things like desktop settings and security policies.

In general, these advanced features are defined and maintained by experienced network administrators over larger networks, and some of these facilities specifically require a Client/Server type of network arrangement in order to function correctly (see page 11).

As we are only concerned with Peer-to-Peer networking in this book, most of these facilities are beyond our scope. However, these parameters can be useful in organising the way the network appears on the desktop, and as such we will look at the basic configuration procedure for defining the computer name and workgroup settings.

Readers who wish to look at the more advanced possibilities will find useful information by installing the Windows Resource Kit from the \tools\reskit\setup.exe on the Windows 98 CD-ROM .

Names

Each individual computer must be assigned a unique 'name'. This 'name' is then associated with the Ethernet address, and provides a useful way to identify the computer to the network system as well as to the user without the user having to use complex coding systems (eg, 'my_computer' is a lot easier to use on a daily basis than 'F8F765B00-2256#').

This 'name' must be unique on the network and consist of alphanumeric characters with no spaces.

Workgroups

The 'workgroup' parameter is simply a convenient method for grouping PCs that are related in some way. This might be either by function (eg, 'Marketing') or by location (eg, 'Biology Lab'). This naming system can be useful for locating resources quickly across a network: when browsing a network on the desktop, the workgroups appear as separate entities which can then be used to access resources on individual computers within that workgroup.

Changing Names and Workgroups

As previously mentioned, these parameters were originally set when Windows 98 was originally installed on each individual PC. These installations may well have been performed by different people at different times, and with no anticipation of future network connections.

To change these parameters proceed as follows:

1 Open the Control Panel, and double-click 'Network' as before to open the Network configuration window.

2 Click on the 'Identification' tab at the top of the window.

'Computer' and 'Workgroup' names can be up to 15 alphanumeric characters long, and can contain the following:!@#$%^&()-_'{}.~

3 Enter unique 'Computer' name.

4 Enter appropriate 'Workgroup' name.

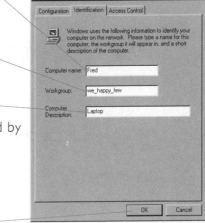

5 Enter a brief description if required, using up to 48 characters. This is not used by the network system, but is used by certain network monitoring utilities.

6 Click 'OK'.

Installing File and Printer Sharing

The final configuration setting that is required before our Windows 98 networking system can be fully implemented is to enable File and Printer Sharing. This will allow other users on the network to access files on your PC hard disk and printers attached to your PC, subject to other security allowances covered later.

To enable this proceed as follows:

1 Open the Control Panel, and double-click 'Network' as before to open the Network configuration window.

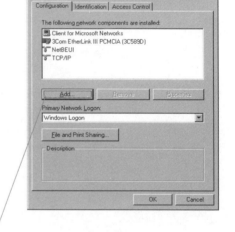

2 Check the list for an entry 'File and printer sharing for Microsoft Networks'.

3 If not present, click 'Add'.

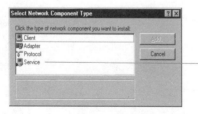

4 From the window that appears, double-click 'Service'.

...cont'd

5 From the list of
Network Clients,
select 'File and
printer sharing for
Microsoft
Networks'.

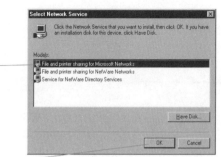

6 Click on 'OK'.

7 Click on 'File and Print
Sharing' in the 'Network'
window.

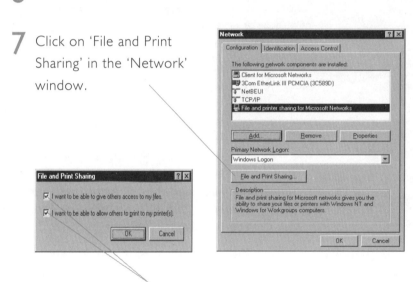

8 Ensure that both 'I want to give others access to my
files' and 'I want to be able to allow others to print to
my printer(s)' are checked.

9 Click on 'OK' and then click on 'OK' in the 'Network'
window. This being the final setting, when prompted to
restart Windows 98, answer 'Yes'.

Share Level Security

Now that we have established the necessary hardware and software links between the PCs on the network, it is potentially possible for all users on the network to gain access to all of the file, printer, and other resources available on the network.

A 'resource' can be any disk drive, directory, file, or peripheral device such as a printer or modem that is attached via a PC interface to the network.

In order to turn this potential into reality, each individual resource that is intended to be accessible needs to be designated as 'shared' across the network (ie, access cannot be facilitated to a specific resource until that resource has been identified as available to the network).

Access to each resource can be defined in a number of different ways, depending on the level and type of security that is required.

Once a resource is defined as 'shared', it can then be further defined as 'changeable' or not (ie, the resource may only be available to 'read from' and not 'write to'). The resource can also be protected from unauthorised access if required by defining a password for that resource.

A resource can be defined as 'shared' at various levels as indicated above. If you make an entire disk drive available as 'shared' then all of the directories and files in that disk drive automatically become available. If, however, you only require certain directories on a disk drive be available across the network, then the entire disk must be defined as 'unshared' but with each individual directory that is intended to be accessible being defined as 'shared' separately. The point is that having defined a resource as 'shared' at a high level, you cannot then define portions of that shared resource as 'unshared'.

Of the three main different types of sharing, we will cover disk-based sharing (ie, drives, directories and files) and printer sharing here, and look at configuring external resource sharing in a later chapter.

Disk-based Sharing

To enable sharing of a particular disk-based resource (ie, a disk drive, directory, or file), proceed as follows. We will assume that we are enabling the highest level of access – the main disk drive:

Don't worry if the view within the 'My Computer' window does not look the same as pictured here. You can change the way that the items are presented by clicking on 'View' and then selecting either 'Large' or 'Small Icons', 'List' or 'Details'.

1 From the Windows 98 Desktop, double-click the 'My Computer' icon.

2 Select the resource that you wish to enable for sharing. For directories and files, double-click again.

3 Right-click on the resource and then click on 'Sharing'.

4 Select the 'Shared As' option.

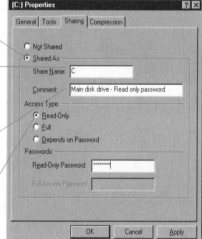

5 Enter an alternative name for the shared resource if required. This will be the main reference name. You may add a comment if you wish.

When assigning names to a resource, it is sometimes a good idea to include details of the location of the resource (eg, 'John – Marketing' or 'Laserprinter – Reception'). This 'What/Where' approach can be useful when managing resources.

6 For limited access with no password, select 'Read only'. If you wish to restrict 'Read only' access you can enter a 'Read only' password in the box provided. Click 'OK'. If you specify a password for 'Read only' access, you will then be prompted to confirm this.

Share Level Security...cont'd

7 If full access is required, select 'Full'. Once again, if you require a password restriction to full access you can specify this in the box provided. Click 'OK'. If you specified a password, you will be prompted to confirm this.

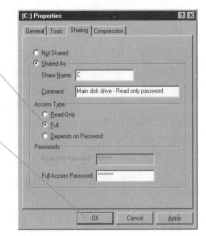

8 You also have the option to control which type of access is granted depending on different passwords. If you select 'Depends on Password' you can then enter two different passwords. When access to this resource is subsequently requested, the type of access granted will depend on which of

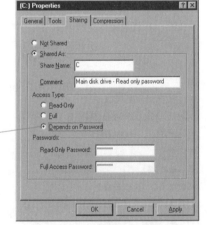

the two passwords was entered. This can be useful, for example if the 'Read only' password is given to users of a particular resource, whilst the 'Full' access password is given to managers of that resource. Once again, on clicking 'OK' you will be prompted to confirm both passwords.

...cont'd

Printer Sharing

The procedure for sharing printers is slightly different from that involving disk-based resources. Enabling printer sharing across a network involves two steps. Firstly the printer must be defined as 'shared' on the PC to which it is attached. This printer then becomes a 'network' printer.

Then the network printer must be added to the list of available printers on any remote PCs (ie, those that wish to access the network printer over the network).

The first step is similar to the procedure involved when sharing a disk-based resource, as follows:

 Assigning a network printer may add to the load on the processor within the attached PC. If you anticipate a heavy printer load onto the network printer, either attach this printer to a PC that is not otherwise heavily used, or spread the load by assigning several printers as shared.

| On the PC to which the printer is physically connected, click 'Start', go to 'Settings' and then click on 'Printers'.

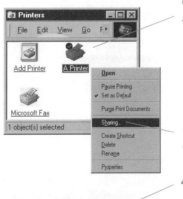

2 Right-click on the printer that you wish to share. If no printers are available, you will need to define one using the 'Add Printer' wizard.

3 Click on 'Sharing'.

4 Click on 'Shared As:'. You can then enter a name for your network printer.

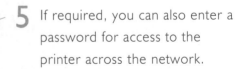

5 If required, you can also enter a password for access to the printer across the network.

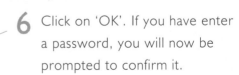

6 Click on 'OK'. If you have enter a password, you will now be prompted to confirm it.

Share Level Security...cont'd

Having defined a printer as 'shared' on the PC to which it is attached, we must then add this printer to the list of available printers on each PC that wishes to gain access to the 'shared' network printer.

| On each PC that requires access to the network printer, click 'Start', go to 'Settings' and then click on 'Printers'.

2 Double-click 'Add Printer'. This will start the Add Printer Wizard. Click 'Next >' on the opening window.

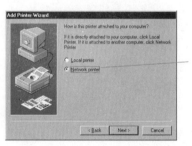

3 Select 'Network printer', and then click 'Next>'.

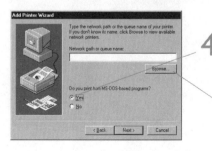

4 Select 'Yes' in answer to 'Do you print from MS-DOS based programs'. Then click 'Browse'.

...cont'd

5 You will then see a view of the network presented in the 'Browse for Printer' window. If the network setup has gone smoothly so far, this will include the name of the computer to which the network printer is attached. Otherwise you will need to refer to 'Troubleshooting the Network Setup'. Click on the '+' next to this to reveal the attached devices.

6 Select the network printer and click 'OK'. The network path will then be entered into the text box in the 'Add Printer Wizard' window. Click 'Next>'.

7 Having selected the 'Yes' option in step 4, you will now be prompted to click on a 'Capture Printer Port' button. This is necessary because programs that run under a DOS window from within Windows 98 behave slightly differently to those running directly under Windows 98 with regards to printer output, and we need to configure for this possibility. Click on this button.

 **You can gain access to a network printer from a PC that already has a printer attached, giving you a choice of printers. In this case Step 8 will suggest a different LPT port to the one which is currently attached to the local printer.**

8 An LPT port assignment will be suggested based on the current local printer configuration. Click 'OK' to accept this, or change the setting using the drop down dialogue. Then click 'Next >'.

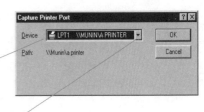

Share Level Security...cont'd

You can also configure Windows 98 to share a fax service across a network. See Chapter 7, page 135 for details.

9 You now need to specify a driver for the printer. If your printer model is available from the list, then select this. Otherwise, insert the manufacturer's installation disk into the appropriate

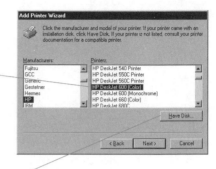

drive and click on 'Have Disk' to install. Once the correct driver is available, click on 'Next>'.

10 You are now asked to supply a name for the network printer. This can be any name and might usefully include details of the printer location. You can also choose to set the

network printer as the default printer or not. This may depend on whether or not you already have a local printer attached to the PC concerned. Once you have made the appropriate selections and/or entries, click 'Next>'.

11 You are asked if you wish to print a test page. I suggest you answer 'No' at this stage; we can test it later! Click 'Finish'. You may be prompted to insert the Windows 98 CD into the CD drive.

A Printer

Once the network printer has been configured, it will appear in the 'Printer' control window with a network attachment as shown.

Managing the Network

In this chapter, we will examine the various Windows 98 utilities available for browsing and managing the resources on the network. We will also look at the Windows 98 network message utility, WinPopup.

Covers

Chapter Five

Network Neighborhood

One of the most useful tools for browsing the network is the Network Neighborhood utility (we will use the American spelling of 'neighbourhood' as it appears in the program, to avoid confusion), which is provided with Windows 98, and is available from the desktop. This utility will allow you to view and access all of the resources that have been defined as 'shared' on the network, including hard drives, directories, files, and other external resources such as printers.

The program is very similar in many respects to the Windows 98 Explorer file manager: the main difference is that Network Neighborhood will only display 'shared' network resources, rather than displaying all of the directories and files on the local hard disk.

One of the disadvantages of the Network Neighborhood utility is that the icon is normally present on the desktop view, which means that any Windows 98 currently maximised must be minimised so that the desktop view becomes available. This can be resolved by clicking on the Network Neighborhood icon and holding the mouse button down as you 'drag' the icon from the desktop and 'drop' it into the 'Start' button on the control bar by releasing the mouse button. The Network Neighborhood utility then becomes available from the 'Start' menu.

On starting the Network Neighborhood utility, you will see something like this:

The 'View' command can be used to display or hide the 'Toolbar' and 'Status Bar' in the window.

The PCs attached to the network are displayed.

Once the 'Toolbar' is displayed, you can also change the appearance of the displayed resources by clicking on one of the last four buttons on the Toolbar as follows:

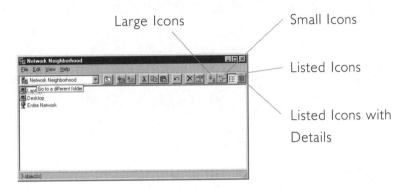

Large Icons

Small Icons

Listed Icons

Listed Icons with Details

Double-clicking on any of the shared resources will display the contents of that resource. The result can either appear in the existing window or be displayed in a new window, depending on an 'Option' setting. To change this setting, click on the 'View' command, and select 'Options' from the menu. Under the 'Folder' tag, you can select either of the 'Browse folders using a single window' or 'Browse folders using separate Windows 98' options.

Other buttons presented on the Toolbar allow you to use the standard features that you find in most Windows 98 applications (ie, Cut, Copy, Paste, Undo, Delete, and Properties). You will also find the 'Up One Level' button, which allows you to quickly move up the resource hierarchy with a single mouse click.

You will also find the standard 'Right Mouse Button' features that are generally available in other Windows 98 based applications.

One additional feature that may be useful within the Network Neighborhood utility is the ability to 'Map' networked hard drives to new drive mappings. You may be familiar with the normal drive mappings for floppy and hard disk drives:

- 'A:' is the first floppy disk drive
- 'B:' is the second floppy disk drive if available
- 'C:' is the local hard disk drive
- 'D:' is the CD-ROM drive if available

Network Neighborhood allows you to allocate additional mapping references to the available networked hard drives.

This can be useful to avoid confusion, for instance, between the local 'C:' drive on your PC, and the 'C:' drive on a networked PC.

You can 'map' the reference to the remote 'C:' drive, for example, as the 'E:' drive. References to the 'C:' drive then refer only to your local hard disk, and references to the 'E:' drive are then directed specifically to the remote 'C:' drive.

Mapping drives is achieved as follows:

1 From the initial Network neighborhood view, double-click on the PC icon that contains the drive you wish to map to.

2 Right-click on the drive that you wish to map to, and then click on 'Map Network Drive'.

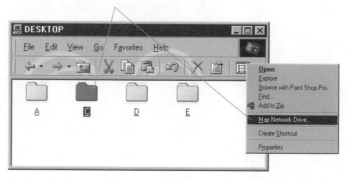

3 Click on the drop-down menu arrow to reveal a list of available mappings.

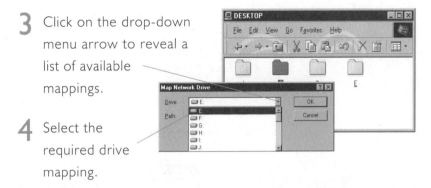

4 Select the required drive mapping.

5 Click on 'Reconnect at Logon' to make this mapping permanent, then click OK.

A new window will appear showing the contents of the drive and its new drive mapping. In this example the 'C:' drive on the 'Desktop' PC has been mapped to drive 'E:' and so the reference in the control bar describes 'C on 'Desktop' (E:)'. Any references made to Drive E: will now be pointed to this network drive.

Disconnecting a network drive mapping is done from the Desktop as follows:

1 From the Desktop, double-click on 'My Computer'.

2 Right-click on the mapping.

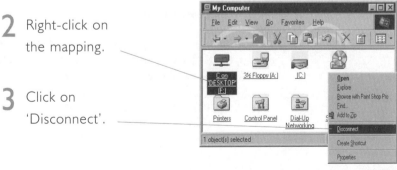

3 Click on 'Disconnect'.

Net View

Net View is a simple DOS based utility which enables you to quickly list the network PCs within a specified workgroup, or to list the shared resources on a specified network PC.

This utility can be run from the 'Start' button on the Windows 98 control bar. Click on 'Start' and then 'Run', and type **net view /?** and click OK.

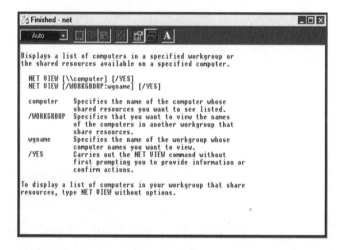

This shows the various command options, displayed in a DOS window.

Thus, using our example network setup, typing **net view / workgroup:workgroup** in the Run dialogue box and clicking OK displays a DOS window containing a list of the PCs contained in that workgroup. You should simply replace the latter 'workgroup' with one of your own workgroup names.

Again, using our example setup, typing net view \\desktop in the 'Run' dialogue and clicking OK will display a list of shared resources on the 'Desktop' PC.

This utility is useful for quickly checking that the network is operational and that the expected resources are available.

Net Watcher

The Net Watcher program is probably the most useful of the Windows 98 network utilities in terms of managing the network. Net Watcher can be used to perform the following functions:

- Showing all shared resources on a PC
- Showing all users connected to a particular resource.
- Showing all opened files on the network
- Closing shared files
- Adding and closing shared resources
- Disconnecting users from a shared resource

Like Net View, Net Watcher can be run from the 'Run' dialogue within the 'Start' menu. It can also be accessed from within the Network Neighborhood utility.

To run Net Watcher from the 'Run' dialogue, click on 'Start' in the Windows 98 control bar, and then 'Run'. Type **netwatch** in the 'Run' dialogue and click OK. If the Toolbar is not visible in the new window, click on 'View' and select 'Toolbar' from the drop-down menu.

Net Watcher needs to be installed as a Windows 98 accessory. If it does not appear to be available, then install it from the Windows 98 CD via 'Start > Settings > Control Panel > AddRemove Programs > Windows Setup > System Tools'.

1 Click on the 'Select Server' button on the Toolbar.

2 Enter the name of the network PC that you wish to monitor, or select 'Browse' and select from the list of network PCs. Click OK.

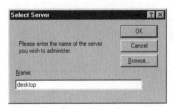

Using our example setup (ie, choosing to monitor 'Desktop') you will see a window similar to the one below.

On the Toolbar, there are three highlighted buttons which give us different views of the 'Desktop' PC, and allow us to monitor three different aspects of this network PC as follows:

1 Users connected.

2 Resources available.

3 Files opened.

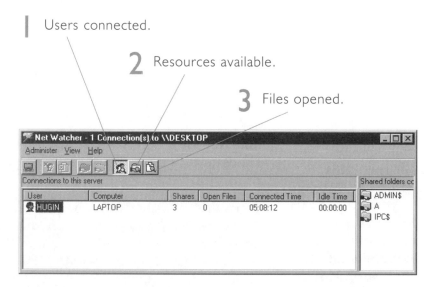

From the 'Show Users' view, shown above, we can see that user 'Hugin' is connected to the 'Desktop' PC from the 'Laptop' PC. This view also allows the disconnection of other users to the 'Desktop' PC.

Clicking on the second button, that is the 'Show Shared Folders' button, we see the following view:

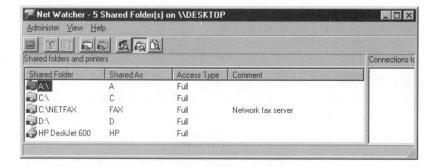

...cont'd

This view shows the list of shared resources available on the 'Desktop' PC and gives details of shared name, access type and any comments.

Selecting any of the available resources will display the name of any network PCs that are connected to that specific resource in the right-hand column.

From this view, we can also see that the Add Share and Stop Sharing buttons have become available.

Add Share   Stop Sharing

Clicking on the 'Add Share' button allows the addition of further shared folders from the 'Desktop' PC. A dialogue box appears requesting a path to the folder to be shared, or offering the 'Browse' facility.

Similarly, clicking the 'Stop Sharing' button allows an existing shared resource to be closed.

Both of these facilities are restricted to folders only, and do not extend to external resources such as printers, etc.

WinPopup

The WinPopup utility allows simple text messages to be sent from one user on the network to another, or to several users contained within a specific workgroup. The Winpopup utility must be running on all PCs on the network for the messages to be sent and received correctly. The best way to ensure this is to setup the Winpopup utility to run as a 'StartUp' program when Windows 98 is first run. Consult the Windows 98 documentation to do this.

Winpopup can be run by typing 'winpopup' from the Start > Run dialogue. A small window will appear as below:

Clicking on the 'envelope' icon on the toolbar will start a new message window.

 Win Popup needs to be installed as a Windows 98 accessory. If it does not appear to be available, then install it from the Windows 98 CD via 'Start > Settings > Control Panel > AddRemove Programs > Windows Setup > System Tools'.

1 Click to send a message.

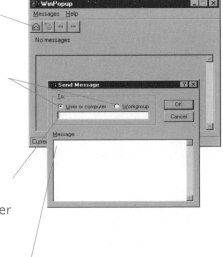

2 Select either 'User or computer' to send to an individual or 'Workgroup' to send messages to all users within the workgroup.

3 Enter the name of the user or the name of the computer or workgroup.

4 Enter the text of the message to be sent, and then click 'OK'.

On sending the message across the network, the Winpopup utility will automatically display the message received by the remote PC or PCs, provided the default settings have not been changed. Clicking on 'Messages > Options' from the toolbar displays options to play a sound when the message arrives, or to disable the automatic display.

Internet Access – Hardware

In this chapter, we will be looking at the various methods of connecting to the Internet. For the time being we will concentrate on the process of setting up the hardware that you might use to connect to the Internet, leaving the business of actually setting up and configuring an Internet account to Chapter Seven.

Covers

Chapter Six

Types of Internet Access

This book is mainly concerned with describing systems for networked users, but here we will also look at providing Internet access for the single user (access to the Internet by a single user may be all that is required, regardless of whether this is from a networked PC or from a stand-alone PC).

Connecting to the Internet is simply a process of allowing your computer to communicate with another specialised computer that is dedicated to providing this service and is permanently connected to the Internet. This specialised remote computer is normally provided by an Internet Service Provider or ISP (we will look at different types of ISPs in Chapter Seven). As the overwhelming majority of Internet communication is via the TCP/IP protocol, you must also be using this protocol in order to establish a communication channel with the Internet via an ISP.

 The TCP/IP protocol, standing for Transmission Control Protocol / Internet Protocol, is the international standard for Internet communications (see page 15).

There are three main types of hardware that are commonly used to connect to the Internet. The choice of which type best suits your needs will depend primarily on how fast you want your connection to operate at, and whether or not you require access for a single user or for a group of users on a network.

The three types are as follows:

• Modem Access – Single user

• ISDN Access – Single user

• ISDN Access – Multiple users

Modem Access
The modem is probably the most common means of allowing communication between remote computers.

This is largely due to the modem's ability to use the public telephone system to transmit and receive digital information.

The term 'Modem' refers to a process known as 'Modulate/ Demodulate' and is simply a cutdown means of expressing a conversion process.

The modulation/demodulation process is the means by which digital information from a computer is converted into a form that can be transmitted over the public telephone network, and then converted back again into a digital signal that can be understood by a computer at the receiving end.

Using the modem to connect to the Internet requires a connection through the public telephone network. This means that the connection needs to be set up by a dial-up process similar to that used when dialling a telephone number in the usual way.

A modem can normally only be used to connect a single computer to another single remote computer. Software does exist that enables many computers to access a modem connected to a single PC over a network, but this is not a very elegant solution and generally requires some fairly complex setting up.

Using the public telephone system, which was originally designed to only carry voice signals, means that the speed at which a converted digital signal can be carried is limited. Modern techniques have been able to increase this speed over recent years, but the limitations imposed by the telephone system still remain.

The main advantage of using a modem connection to connect to the Internet is that of a relatively low cost, both in terms of hardware and connection charges. Most Internet Service Providers are now able to supply Internet access via a local number.

The disadvantages of using a modem connection are those of limited speed; of delays in connecting due to the time required to dial-up the connection number; and the ability to only provide a one-to-one connection.

ISDN – Overview

The term ISDN is short for Integrated Services Digital Network. ISDN was developed to overcome the shortcomings of the standard public telephone system when used to connect remote computers together.

Essentially ISDN provides the means to allow digital communication to occur directly without first having to be converted (modulated/demodulated) to the type of signal normally associated with the public telephone system; hence the 'Digital Network'.

The 'Integrated Services' means that the ISDN system can carry all types of digital signal. This means that a number of different media types can be transmitted simultaneously. Thus a digitised voice signal can share the same channel as a computer data signal or a digitised video signal, allowing several 'virtual' connections to occur at the same time. It is therefore possible to hold a conversation using ISDN involving live audio and video signals at the same time as transmitting computer files.

ISDN networks have gradually evolved over recent years to encompass most of the developed world, and are being used extensively by multinational corporations to transfer large amounts of data across continents, and to provide 'real-time' multi-channel video/audio conferencing facilities.

More recently still, the cost of providing ISDN connectivity has dropped considerably, allowing small and medium sized businesses to benefit from the enhanced capabilities.

The major benefit of using ISDN to connect to the Internet is the considerable increase in data speed, but also the ability to establish and to drop a connection almost instantaneously. This results not only in faster access times, but allows the connection to be made and dropped automatically as the need arises, giving the user the impression of a permanent connection.

There are two types of ISDN hardware available for connecting to the Internet:

ISDN – Single User Access

The first allows an ISDN connection from a single PC and is known as an ISDN Terminal Adapter. This kind of Internet access is most suitable for a single PC user who requires either a high speed connection or rapid access times. ISDN Terminal Adapters are available either as external devices that connect to the PC via a cable interface, or as internal PC cards.

ISDN – Multiple User Access

You may come across a device known as an ISDN Bridge/Router. These devices offer an additional 'Bridging' capability allowing two or more remote LANs to be connected together across the ISDN Network so that they appear to the users at both sites to be one single LAN.

The second type is known as an ISDN Router, and allows access for many PCs on a network to ISDN services. The ISDN Router is connected to the LAN in the same way that a PC is connected, and simply behaves as an additional shared network resource.

An ISDN Router is so called because it has the capability to identify the destination address of incoming TCP/IP packets and assign the appropriate Ethernet addresses. The TCP/IP packets can then be delivered directly to the appropriate PC over the Ethernet LAN. This also means that many PCs can effectively share the ISDN resource so that multiple PC users on the same LAN can appear to access the Internet simultaneously.

Apart from the previously stated advantages of ISDN access, this routing capability can also provide other advantages. There are the obvious cost advantages of not having to have individual modems attached to each computer on the LAN, with the associated line hardware and rental costs.

Also the single access point and routing capabilities of an ISDN Router means that many of the security issues associated with Internet access become easier to manage. ISDN Routers are often available with these enhanced security features built-in.

Types of Modem

The types of modem that are available for PC users can broadly be defined as the following:

- Internal or External Modems

- Modems with or without Fax capabilities

- Modems with different data speed capabilities

External versus Internal Modems

External modems are those that connect to the PC via an interface cable, usually to one of the Serial Communications Ports available on your PC.

External modems hold an advantage over internal modems in that they normally display a range of status indicator lights, which can make the process of troubleshooting errors easier (provided you understand the details of serial communication protocols). In the days when modem configuration was something of an art, these indicators would prove invaluable. More recently the process of modem configuration has been largely automated, and so the need for this kind of information has diminished. The fact that external modems also need their own power supply means an increased cost, and so in most cases the benefits of an external modem have been outweighed in favour of internal ones.

An internal modem is fitted into one of the internal card slots within your PC. Internal modems can be of various types depending on the type of PC architecture that your system contains, similar to those described for PC Network Interface Cards (see page 48).

Both types are generally fitted with an internal speaker so that you can choose to monitor the sounds associated with the process of establishing a dial-up connection.

The main disadvantage of using a PC based Fax system is that your PC must be switched on with the fax software running in order to receive faxes.

Fax Modems

Most of the popularly available modems include the capability to send and receive fax communications. The necessary software needed to implement this capability on your PC is often also provided, albeit frequently in a rather primitive form.

Different Speeds

The speed capabilities of a modem are indicated by its 'baud' rate. This term refers to the number of signal changes that occur per second at the output of the modem and is used as a measure of 'raw' output speed. The amount of actual data or 'bits' per second (bps) depends on the type and degree of signal encoding that occurs, and so the baud rate does not always indicate the true data rate. However, it is true to say that the higher the baud rate, the higher the theoretical data rate. In many cases the data rate of a modem is now quoted in 'bps' to avoid this confusion.

Until recently it was common to find modems available as either 9600 baud or 14400 baud. Now, with advances in modem technology it is more common to find modems available as 28800 or 33600 bps. More recently still, modems with speeds up to 56Kbs are now available.

Modem Installation

As described in the previous section, external modems are now relatively rare, and so we will be concentrating on installing and configuring an internal modem. As there is also little fundamental difference between modems, we will take a generalised look at modem installation without referring to a specific modem vendor.

Before installing a modem, it may be necessary to select a series of 'jumper' settings on the modem card. This will depend on the specific modem that you are installing. Many vendors allow these settings to be made via the accompanying software, eliminating the need to set these manually on the modem card itself. If this is the case then simply install the modem as indicated below.

If these settings do need to be set manually, then follow the instructions in the manufacturer's instruction manual to do this. Often the 'jumpers' will be set to default settings at the factory.

 If you are unsure about which modem settings to use, try Com=3 and IRQ=5, but only if you do not have a second printer attached to LPT=2.

These settings will define two main elements: the 'Com Port' setting, and the 'Interrupt' (or IRQ) setting. The important thing about these settings is that they must be unique to the modem. The processor uses the combination of these settings to communicate with the modem. All of the devices attached to your PC, such as the mouse, CD ROM, or Sound card will already be using some of the available settings to communicate with the processor, and it is important that you do not duplicate any settings that are used by other devices.

Be careful to make a note of any settings that you select as you will need these later.

Once any manual settings that you may need to make have been made, install the modem into the PC by following the instructions on page 50 for the NIC installation. Installation of any PC card into your PC will follow this same procedure.

Modem Configuration

Once the modem has been installed in your PC, you can begin configuring Windows 98 to use the modem. There are several ways in which you can approach this.

If your modem is identified as a Windows 98 'Plug and Play' compatible device then you can get Windows 98 to recognise and configure the modem more or less automatically.

If you do not have the manufacturer's installation disk, then you can usually configure the modem using one of Windows 98 'standard' modem drivers appropriate to the speed of the modem. If you have the manufacturer's installation disk, then you can use this to supply the modem specific drivers to Windows 98, allowing you to fully utilise any specialised features that your modem can support.

Many modem suppliers now supply installation software that will fully automate the whole process. If this is the case, try installing the modem using the manufacturer's disk and instruction manual in the first place.

The following procedure therefore is intended only as a guide to the installation process, and to help you address any problems.

1   Click on Start/Settings/Control Panel and then double-click 'Add New Hardware'.

2   The 'Add New Hardware Wizard' will appear. Click 'Next>' and then 'Next>' again.

3   The Wizard will ask you if you want Windows 98 to search for new hardware. If your modem is 'Plug and Play' compatible then select 'Yes (Recommended)'. Windows 98 will then automatically configure the modem. You can try this process anyway if you are not sure Whether your modem is 'Plug and Play' compatible or not. If not, select 'No'. Click 'Next>'.

Modem Configuration...cont'd

4 The Wizard will then ask you to select the type of hardware that you wish to install. Select 'Modem' from the list (scroll down) and click 'Next>'.

5 Once again the Wizard will give you the option to automatically detect the modem. Again, if you wish you can allow Windows 98 to examine each 'Com Port' for an attached modem and then attempt an automatic configuration. Otherwise select 'Don't detect my modem'. Click 'Next>'.

6 The Install New Modem window will appear.

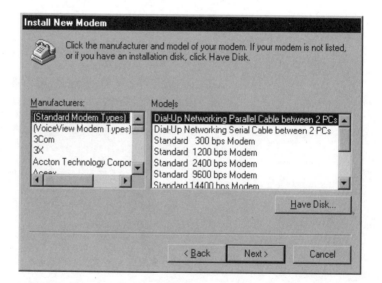

If your modem manufacturer is listed in the 'Manufacturers' list, you can select this. Selecting a manufacturer will produce a list of 'Models'. If your modem model is available, then select it from the list.

If not, then you can select 'Standard Modem Types' from the 'Manufacturers' list, and then select the speed of modem that matches yours.

The third option is to click 'Have Disk'. This will then prompt you to insert the manufacturer's disk into the A: drive and will load the correct driver from this disk.

7 Having selected a modem driver using one of these options, click 'Next >'.

8 From the list of communication ports presented, select the one that either you have manually configured your modem to use using the jumper settings, or a Com port that is not already assigned to another device.

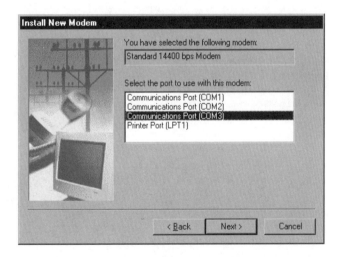

Then click on 'Next >'. Windows 98 will then attempt to load the software driver that you have selected, and configure for the port that you have indicated. If this is successful, the wizard will report this and ask you to click 'Finish'. You will then be returned to the Control Panel window.

Checking the Modem

You can check the configuration of the modem as follows:

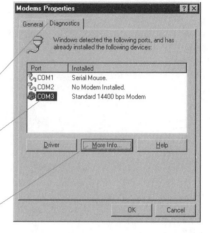

1   From the Control Panel, double-click on 'Modems'.

2   Select the 'Diagnostics' tab at the top of the window.

3   From the list of installed ports, select the one attached to the modem and then click 'More Info...'.

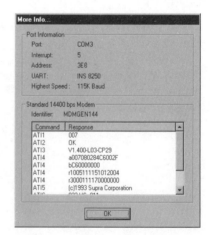

4   After a few seconds, during which Windows 98 sends a series of commands to the modem, a 'More Info...' window will appear. This will show the complete details of the modem configuration together with all of the command results.

If the diagnostics test proceeds smoothly without reporting any errors, then your modem installation has been successful. Otherwise you will need to check that the various modem settings are correct.

Types of ISDN Hardware

There are two types of hardware that will allow ISDN access to the Internet.

The first provides a service similar to the modem access in that it allows a single PC to connect to the Internet via an ISDN link. This type of connection requires an ISDN Terminal Adapter, which is usually installed as an internal PC card. It allows faster access than through a modem link, but is limited in that only one PC can be connected (although software is available to extend this capability).

 As ISDN is capable of carrying several types of digital signal, ISDN hardware often includes the capability to plug in digital phones and faxes, as well as being able to connect to data networks.

ISDN links can better be used to connect a number of PCs to the Internet at the same time by 'routing' the connection via an ISDN Router. The ISDN router is connected on one port to the Internet, and on another to an Ethernet network. The ISDN router then provides a means to determine which IP packets are destined for which Ethernet address and thereby to individual PCs on the network. This process of 'routing' IP packets from an ISDN Internet connection to specific PCs on a network is the main job of the ISDN router. Multiple PCs can then effectively share the capacity of the faster ISDN channel.

As we are dealing primarily with networks, we will look specifically at this type of 'routed' ISDN connection.

Unlike most types of modem based dial-up IP accounts, the business of setting up and supplying ISDN accounts by those Internet Service Providers that can provide this facility is still very much in development. This is particularly the case with smaller accounts (aimed at between two and fifty users on a network) rather than 'corporate' type accounts. The numerous types of ISDN router available, and their various approaches to the configuration process, further complicates the issue.

For these reasons, we will concentrate on a single popular UK based Internet Service Provider with ISDN capability, and look specifically at setting up two of the more popular ISDN routers.

ISDN Installation

To install an ISDN Internet access link capability to your network you will need the following:

- An ISDN line connection

- An ISDN Internet Service Provider (ISP) account

- An ISDN Router

- A connection to the LAN (for the router)

- A 'Null Modem' serial connection cable if using the alternative router option (see below)

The ISDN Router acts as an interface between the network and the ISP ISDN link. As such it requires an ISDN connection the ISP on the one hand, and an ethernet interface to the network on the other.

The ISDN connection to the ISP will require the installation of an ISDN line. In the UK this will normally be supplied and installed by British Telecom PLC according to a number of different pricing structures depending on the length of the supply contract and the degree of free call time included in the package.

A Coax BNC connection or an RJ45 connection to an Ethernet hub will connect the ISDN Router to your Ethernet network as an additional ethernet address. When deciding upon the specific model of ISDN Router to purchase, remember that it will need to support the correct type of network interface for your network.

The alternative ISDN Router that we will be looking at will also require an additional type of 'serial' connection that will connect a PC to the ISDN Router via its 'serial' or 'Com' port. A 'Serial Null Modem' cable with appropriate connectors at either end will be needed to configure and control the ISDN Router.

The 'serial' port on both the Router and the PC is normally a '9 pin D-Type' connector, although on some older PCs this may be a '25 pin D-Type' connector. A suitable 'Serial Null Modem' cable can be purchased from most high street PC shops. The various combinations of 9 or 25 pin and male or female connectors can be confusing; make sure you specify the one suitable to your PC and ISDN Router and also ensure that it is of the 'Null Modem' type.

The 'Demon' ISDN Account

Once you have an ISDN line installed, you will then be in a position to set up an ISDN Internet access account with an ISDN capable ISP. One of the popular ISDN capable UK ISPs is Demon Internet Ltd.

Demon are able to ease the process of setting up your ISDN Internet access by providing a package that includes a fully configured ISDN Router.

There are then a number of options available within the Demon ISDN account pricing structure which allow the supply of any number of IP addresses, suitable to the size of your network requirements.

Once you have signed up to one of the Demon ISDN account options and been supplied with the pre-configured ISDN Router, the process of setting up the Internet connection is straightforward: connect the router to the network and to the ISDN line, and then configure the Windows 98 setup on all of your attached network PCs with the appropriate protocol drivers and individual IP address settings.

In the following sections we will look at setting up an alternative to the Demon ISDN Router option. Then in Chapter Seven we will deal with the necessary Windows 98 protocol driver configuration and IP setup for both router options.

The 3Com ISDN Router

If you choose to purchase your own ISDN Router independent of your ISDN capable ISP, you will need to configure this yourself.

One such supplier of popular ISDN Routers is 3Com. The 'Office Connect' range of 3Com Routers provide a 'Quick Configuration' utility which eases the configuration process.

We will now look at configuring the 3Com Office Connect Remote 510 ISDN Router in some detail.

The Serial Control Interface

Before we look at the specifics of setting up the 3Com ISDN Router, we first need to establish the serial connection control interface that will allow access to the configuration parameters held within the router. This is done using the 'Hyper Terminal' utility that is part of Windows 98, and the 'Null Modem' serial connection cable.

 If the Windows 'Hyper Terminal' utility proves unstable, then use one of the many other popular communications packages available, such as Procomm or Telix.

Before you can run the Windows 98 Hyper Terminal utility you need to check that it was installed during the Windows 98 setup procedure. You will find out by clicking 'Start/ Programs/Accessories' in Windows 98. If the 'Hyper Terminal' utility is not present in the list of Windows 98 Accessories, you will need to install it from your Windows 98 setup disc(s) using the 'Add/Remove Programs' procedure from the 'Control Panel'. If in doubt, refer to a similar procedure for installing the 'Dial-Up Adapter – Installation' in the 'Modem Access – Configuration' section of Chapter Seven.

...cont'd

To establish the serial control interface, proceed as follows:

1 With power 'off' on both devices, connect the 'Null Modem' cable from the serial interface port on your PC (often marked 'COM1') to the serial interface port on the router (marked 'Serial'). The 'Com' port on your PC may be configured as Com1, 2, 3 or 4. You will need to know which 'Com' port settings you are using.

2 Power up the router and the PC and run Windows 98.

3 Click on 'Settings/ Programs/Accessories/ Hyper Terminal'. Then double-click on 'Hypertrm.exe'. A 'New Connection – Hyper Terminal' window will appear containing the following.

4 Enter any Name (eg, '3Com') and click on 'OK'.

5 Click on the drop-down menu for 'Connect using' and select 'Direct to.....' the 'Com' port that you are using to connect to the router. Click OK.

6 Ensure that the settings shown below are selected using the drop-down menus, then click OK. Try clicking on 'Restore Defaults'. This may set all of the parameters for you.

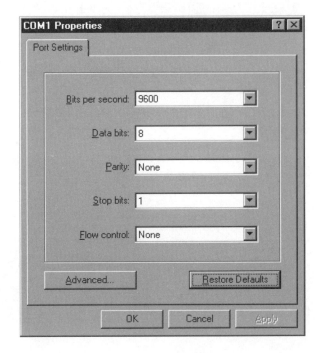

7 Click OK. This will bring up the new Hyper Terminal session. Pressing the 'Enter' key will start the serial command interface session with the 3Com router, and request a password.

8 Enter the default password 'PASSWORD' (in capitals) and press the 'Enter' key. The Main Configuration Menu will then appear as follows, with the cursor blinking at the 'Enter Command' position.

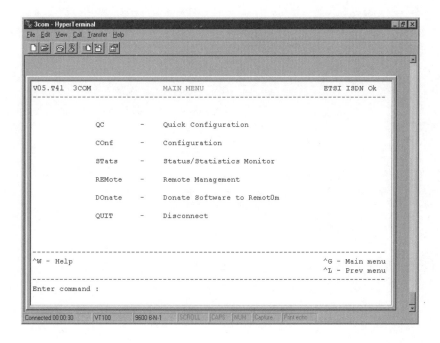

Configuring the 3Com ISDN Router

Now that we have established serial communication with the router configuration interface, we can configure the router. We will be configuring for a Demon ISDN access, but the procedure will be similar for other ISDN capable ISPs.

Your ISP will provide you with the following information:

- An ISDN dial-in number

- A remote IP address

- A login ID

- A login password

Once you have this information you can proceed to configure the 3Com Remote 510s.

1 At the 'Enter Command' prompt, type 'qc na' and press the 'Enter' key.

2 In the 'Unit Parameters' window, enter values as follows, using the up/down arrow keys to move between selections:

Enter any name

```
Unit Name              : 3COM

Unit LAN IP address    : 20.0.0.1

Unit LAN IP mask       : 255.0.0.0

Network Type           : Europe, including UK (ETSI)
```

Enter IP address and mask as shown

Press spacebar to select ISDN type as appropriate

3 Hold down the 'Ctrl' key and then press the 'E' key to enter these settings.

4 At the 'Enter command' prompt, type 'co na' and press 'Enter'. In the 'Edit NAT parameters' window, enter the following details:

Use the spacebar to select 'Enabled'

Enter the 'Remote IP Address' as specified by your ISP here

```
Network Address Translation: ENABLED

NAT IP Address             : 195.11.192.1

NAT Masqueraded Network    : 20.0.0.0
NAT Masqueraded Mask       : 255.0.0.0
```

Enter these as shown

5 Hold down the 'Ctrl' key and then press the 'E' key to enter these settings.

6 At the 'Enter command' prompt, type 'qc in' and then press the 'Enter' key.

7 In the 'Connect to Another PPP IP Router' window, enter the following details.

```
Name of your Internet Provider or remote site  :Demon
ISDN number of the remote unit you want to call:08450798661
Call Type                                       :64K Unrestricted
IP Address of this unit's LAN port              :20.0.0.1
IP Mask of this unit's LAN port                 :255.0.0.0
IP Address of this end of the ISDN link         :UNNUMBERED
IP Address of the remote end of the ISDN link   :UNNUMBERED
IP Mask of the ISDN link                        :UNNUMBERED
IP Address of the remote hosts network          :INTERNET
IP Mask of the remote hosts network             :INTERNET
Manufacturer of remote router                   :DEFAULT
ID to log into remote site                      :login ID
ID for others to log into you                   :UNUSED
PAP Password to log into remote site            :password
PAP Password for others to log into you         :UNUSED
CHAP Password to log into remote site           :UNUSED
CHAP Password for others to log into you        :UNUSED
```

Enter any name here

Enter the ISDN dial-in number here

Enter the 'login ID' here

Enter the 'login password' here

Remember to use the correct case when entering the login ID and password.

If your ISP uses CHAP security control, then enter the password at the 'Control Password to log into remote site' position, rather than at the PAP password position.

8 Hold down the 'Ctrl' key and then press the 'E' key to enter these settings.

9 At the 'Enter command' prompt, type 'sa' and press the 'Enter key. Then type 'reboot y' and press the 'Enter' key.

The rebooting process will reset the 3Com router and store the new configuration before performing a self test.

If you have not already done so, connect the router to the ISDN line using the cable supplied, and to the network via a suitable connector (either a BNC connector to the Coax bus, or an RJ45 cable to an Ethernet hub).

If you now follow the Windows 98 TCP/IP configuration in Chapter Seven for this type of ISDN router, you should now find that the 3Com router functions correctly and connects your networked PCs to the Internet.

However, there are a couple of further modifications you can make at this point which will improve the efficiency of your ISDN link.

Changing the Time-Out Setting

The first involves the amount of time that the ISDN link remains active after any link activity has stopped. This setting is known as the link 'time-out' setting. Adjusting this can reduce the total amount of time spent on-line, and thus reduce your phone bills.

The 3Com default setting for the link time-out is 120 seconds. This can be reduced, but be aware that the time-out needs to be long enough for any response IP packets from the Internet to be able to be returned following an Internet request before the line is shut down. A time-out setting of between 20–60 seconds will probably be about right.

To change the time-out setting proceed as follows:

1 Go to the 'Main Menu' of the 3Com serial command interface. You can do this by pressing and holding down the 'Ctrl' key, and then pressing the 'G' key.

2 At the 'Enter command' prompt, type 'co is auto ip ed' and press 'Enter'.

3 The 'Edit ISDN IP Autocall Address' window will display with the following settings.

```
IP Address      :   0.0.0.0
IP Mask         :   0.0.0.0
Inverse         :   DISABLED
Remote Unit     :   DEMON
Bumpable        :   FALSE
Idle (secs)     :   20
Idle Threshold  :   >0
```

Change the 'Idle' position to your time-out setting

4 Hold down the 'Ctrl' key and then press the 'E' key to enter these settings.

5 At the 'Enter command' prompt, type 'sa' and press the 'Enter key. Then type 'reboot y' and press the 'Enter' key.

You must define the Call Filters exactly as shown, and in the same order. Filters defined in any other order will not function as required.

Adding a Call Filter

One of the problems associated with the Windows 98 networking protocol is that it tends to produce network 'calls' to the 3Com router which cause it to bring up the ISDN link, even though you are not using the Internet.

This can result in excessive phone bills: the router will respond to these calls as long as it is connected to the ISDN line and functioning correctly, a situation which would tend to prevail under normal working conditions.

To prevent the router making these unnecessary connections, you can configure the router to 'filter-out' these network calls as follows:

I At the 'Enter command' prompt at the 'Main Menu', type 'co ro ipf ap' and press 'Enter'.

2 The 'Edit Firewall Entry' will appear. Enter the following details either by typing in for the left hand entries or pressing the spacebar for those on the right. Use the Up/Down keys to move from one entry to the next.

```
Src Address   : 195.11.192.1         Enter the 'Remote IP
Src Mask      : 255.255.255.255      address' here
SrPort(s)  :    0-65535

Dest Address  : 0.0.0.0
Dest Mask     : 0.0.0.0              Enter the 'Mask'
Dest Port(s)  : 0-65535             as shown
```

Set the 'Bidirectional' setting to 'Enable' using the spacebar

```
Type          : ALL

Action        : ACCEPT

Bidirectional : ENABLE

TcpSYN        : DISABLE
```

3 Hold down the 'Ctrl' key and then press the 'E' key to enter these settings.

This is the first filter setting, which will now be displayed in the 'Firewall Configuration' screen as follows (your IP Sources address will be different):

```
V05.T41  3COM              FIREWALL CONFIGURATION              ETSI ISDN Down
-----------------------------------------------------------------------------
                                                              Page No. 1 of 1

Type  Source          Destination          Action  Bidir  Packets
[ALL  195.11.192.1/32  0.0.0.0/0           ACCEPT  TRUE         0]
```

We need to define two more filters as follows:

4 At the 'Enter command' prompt in the 'Firewall Configuration' screen, type 'ap' and press 'Enter'. Then enter the following details as before.

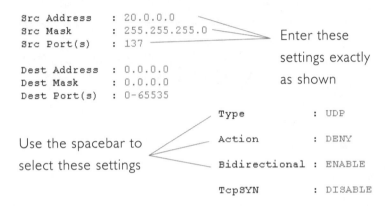

```
Src Address    : 20.0.0.0
Src Mask       : 255.255.255.0
Src Port(s)    : 137

Dest Address   : 0.0.0.0
Dest Mask      : 0.0.0.0
Dest Port(s)   : 0-65535
```

Enter these settings exactly as shown

Use the spacebar to select these settings

```
Type           : UDP
Action         : DENY
Bidirectional  : ENABLE
TcpSYN         : DISABLE
```

5 Once again, hold down the 'Ctrl' key and then press the 'E' key to enter these settings.

6 You will find the second filter now appear in the 'Firewall Configuration' screen. Move the selector down onto this new setting using the 'Down' arrow key, and then type 'ap' and press 'Enter' to define the final filter.

```
Src Address    : 20.0.0.0
Src Mask       : 255.255.255.0
Src Port(s)    : 0-65535

Dest Address   : 0.0.0.0
Dest Mask      : 0.0.0.0
Dest Port(s)   : 0-65535
```

Enter these settings exactly as shown

Set the 'Bidirectional' setting to 'Enable' using the spacebar

```
Type           : ALL
Action         : ACCEPT
Bidirectional  : ENABLE
TcpSYN         : DISABLE
```

7 Hold down the 'Ctrl' key and then press the 'E' key to enter these settings.

8 At the 'Enter command' prompt, type 'sa' and press the 'Enter key. Then type 'reboot y' and press the 'Enter' key.

After rebooting, the 3Com router will now be ready to connect your network to the Internet, after you have configured the Windows 98 TCP/IP protocol drivers as described in the next chapter.

Internet Access – Getting Connected

In this chapter, we will look at the process of getting connected to the Internet. We will first look at choosing a service provider, and then at how to configure Windows 98 for the connection process and the various types of Internet access hardware.

Covers

Chapter Seven

Internet Service Providers

What is the Internet?

Before looking at the various types of Internet Service Providers available, it will be useful here to take a look at what the Internet actually is.

As the Internet has no single geographic centre or administrative body, this question has many different answers depending on your point of view.

In Chapter One we looked at the TCP/IP protocol. It could be argued that, as the Internet Protocol is the single unifying feature of the Internet, the Internet is therefore IP, and vice versa. Others might say that the Internet consists of all of the hardware infrastructure that connects all of the many thousands of computers together and provides the backbone of the Internet system. The average user might simply say that the Internet is a service that can be derived from a number of different sources.

Whatever your perspective, one definition that holds true is that for any resource to be a part of the Internet, it must be available to the rest of the Internet on a more or less continual basis. Thus, any Internet resource must be quickly available on demand, if not actually 'hard wired' to the rest of the Internet.

There is therefore a difference between the casual user of the Internet (ie, someone who uses the Internet resources) and some person or organisation who supplies those resources. In general terms it could be said that the casual user does not actually become a permanent part of the Internet, but merely 'dials-in' to the Internet on a temporary basis.

The casual user therefore needs to be able to access an Internet 'access point' as required. The Internet Service Provider provides this access point either via a local public telephone number, or via an ISDN link. Those that provide more permanent links will effectively allow the end-user to become a true part of the Internet, and to provide Internet services.

We can now turn to the various types of Internet Service Providers.

There are two basic types: those that provide a variety of purely Internet based services (which we will call Internet Access Providers) and those that provide other information services (which are known as Content Providers).

Internet Access Providers

The basic service that any Internet Service Provider (ISP) offers is the means to provide a dial-up link via a publicly available telecommunication service (ie, telephone or ISDN), which supports an IP channel across that link. The ISP then handles the IP packets coming from and going to that link.

In order to support the IP link across the telephone system, an additional protocol is required, which an ISP must also be able to support. This will either be the Point-to-Point Protocol (PPP) or the Serial Line Internet Protocol (SLIP). As PPP has largely replaced SLIP access now, for the following configuration procedures we will assume PPP.

The ISP must also provide a means of resolving what are known as 'Domain Name' address queries. This process will be supplied by the ISP's 'Domain Name Server'. The IP protocol provides a means of converting Domain Names (which for example form part of a URL – see page 165) which people can understand, into IP addresses (eg, 012.345.678.9) which computers can understand. Thus when you type a URL into your web browser, the Domain Name part of the URL must first be converted into its IP address before the web page can be located and delivered to the browser. Each Domain Name is assigned its specific IP address when it is created, and so the process of converting one to the other is simply a matter of looking up its entry in a database. Finding where that particular Domain Name/ IP address relationship is recorded and then using this information to make the correct conversion is the job of the 'Domain Name Server' (DNS).

The minimum basic services that an ISP must provide can be summarised as follows:

- Dial-up access for either analogue (public telephone) or digital (ISDN) telecom links

- Support for the PPP protocol

- Support for handling IP packets

- Access to a Domain Name Server

As these are the basic minimum, most ISPs will provide these as a matter of course and will not necessarily advertise these capabilities.

Internet Access Providers – E-mail Services

Most ISPs will also provide e-mail services. An 'E-mail Server' at the ISP will provide e-mail sending and collection capabilities, similar in effect to that provided by a normal mail Post Box. When you register with an ISP, an e-mail 'account' is set up on the mail server. You will then be able to send e-mail via the ISP using suitable e-mail 'client' software on your PC. Any e-mail that is sent to your e-mail address(es) is collected by the mail server at the ISP, for delivery to you when you are ready.

ISPs will normally provide you with one or more e-mail addresses, depending on the type of account that you select. Many will restrict the number of e-mail addresses that you can use, while a few allow an unlimited number of e-mail addresses. Having several e-mail addresses means that you could, for instance, allocate different addresses to members of your family; or in a small business environment, to members of staff.

Several e-mail accounts will generally operate under a single Internet access account.

Those ISPs that provide an unlimited number of e-mail accounts under a single Internet access account can represent a considerable saving if your organisational needs are for more than just a few e-mail accounts. In these circumstances, consideration needs to be given as to how multiple e-mail addresses are collected and managed at the user end of the Internet link.

 An e-mail 'client' is the e-mail software that resides on the local PC, as opposed to the e-mail 'server' which is located at the ISP end of the Internet link.

Special e-mail software packages which act as local e-mail sorting agents, are available. These act as intermediaries between the ISP's Mail Server and the individual users on a network, and sort incoming e-mail so that e-mail addressed to different addresses is directed over the network to the appropriate e-mail client.

Internet Access Providers – Newsgroups

Most ISPs will also be able to supply access to Newsgroups. As some of the many different areas covered by the thousands of available Newsgroups may be considered of an 'undesirable' nature, some ISPs will block access to these, whilst others allow unlimited access to all available newsgroups. Newsgroups are made available to the user via a 'Newsgroup Server' at the ISP.

Internet Access Providers – Additional Services

Competition between different Internet Access Providers for your Internet account is currently very strong, with new ISPs springing up almost on a daily basis.

This means that many are offering additional services in order to tempt you in their particular direction.

Some examples of the additional services an ISP may offer are as follows:

- Free Web Space – hard Disk space on the ISP's Web Server to host your own web site. For a typical small business site, more than 1Mb is rarely necessary, unless you plan to provide highly detailed product support information or possibly 'E-Commerce' facilities.

A 'hit' will occur on your web site every time a specific piece of information is requested. This can include individual graphics as well as text pages, and so 'hit' statistics need to be properly qualified to give an accurate picture of web site usage.

- Web Site Statistics – the ability to supply various types of web site statistics (eg, to show how many user 'hits' your web site has generated).

- Domain Name Registration Services – registering a unique Domain Name for your organisation's web site. This will reduce a potentially complex web site address (eg, www.ispsite.co.uk/wwwserver companyname /welcome.htm) to one that your customers will remember more easily (eg,www.mycompany.com).

- E-mail Forwarding – this would usually be used in conjunction with a unique Domain Name and allows e-mail sent to a web site address to be redirected or 'forwarded' to a specified e-mail account. For example, e-mail sent from a web page link to support@www.company.com' could be forwarded to 'jbloggs@www.company.com', a member of the technical support team.

- CGI Scripting – the 'Common Gateway Interface' language is a means of allowing information to be collected from a web site user, and then performing some operation using this information. An example might be a form on your web site that invites potential customers to request information leaflets through the post by inputting their contact details. This information is then sent to the ISP Web Server, where the CGI Scripting program compiles the details into an e-mail and sends it to you, as well as returning a dynamic web page to the user's browser, informing them that the operation has been successfully completed.

As designing and implementing CGI scripts requires skilled Internet programmers and access to the core functions of an ISP's Internet server, this kind of facility is usually provided as a set of predefined CGI scripts that perform specific functions. However some ISPs, aimed at supplying professional services to the web developer, allow custom made CGI scripts to be loaded into a restricted area on the ISP's server.

- Fax/E-mail Services – the ability to convert e-mail into a fax transmission. This can save considerably on international fax transmission costs by providing the same capability at the cost of a local call.

- E-Commerce Services – the ability to securely handle cash transactions over the Internet. This would certainly be useful to those wishing to use the Internet to take direct credit card payments for products ordered from a web site.

Content Providers

Internet access is also now frequently available through what would otherwise be suppliers of information services.

Before the Internet became so widely available, several companies set up publicly available computerised information services. By subscribing to these services, users are able to access a wide range of predefined information services from their PC via a modem connection, and using a company specific 'browser' package.

Since the advent of the Internet, these companies now often supply the basic Internet services such as e-mail and web browsing, alongside their own 'content' services.

Costs for these services tend to be higher than for a straight forward Internet access account, and in some cases the development of the proprietary 'browser' tends to lag behind in the race to implement the latest browser 'standards'.

Choosing an ISP

Choosing the right ISP for your needs depends to a large extent upon your specific requirements, especially if you need specialised services like ISDN access or CGI scripting capabilities.

If you plan to upgrade from a Dial-Up connection to an ISDN connection in the future, choose an ISP that is able to provide both. This will avoid having to change your e-mail address when you make the transition.

For a straight forward modem dial-up account with the basic Internet services, you will find that there are many competing suppliers in the marketplace. The following are some points to bear in mind to help you choose between them.

Perhaps the two most important considerations are: the ability of an ISP to provide a free line on-demand, and the speed at which the connection operates once established.

The first consideration is determined by the ratio of available lines into the ISP divided by the number of potential users. When you attempt to dial into an ISP for an Internet connection, you are likely to be competing with other users, especially at busy times of the day. The chances of you getting a free line will be determined by this lines/user ratio. Many ISPs will tell you what this ratio is. A low ratio (eg, 5:1) will mean that you will obtain a line almost every time, or a higher ratio may mean that you may get a 'number unobtainable' tone on occasion, and will need to redial in order to establish a connection.

The speed at which the line operates once connected is not always simply a matter of the speed of your modem. At peak times, or whenever there is a heavy demand, the data rate available to each connected user is regulated, thereby apparently slowing down your connection. The need to do this will in part be determined by the 'trunk' data rate available to the ISP (ie, the kind of telecommunication connection that the ISP has to the rest of the Internet). Thus the ISPs with the larger trunk connections will be able to provide the maximum data speeds to their users more of the time.

Modem Access – Configuration

In Chapter Six we looked at setting up the modem and checking its configuration. Now that we have discussed the business of selecting an ISP, you may be in a position to purchase and set-up an ISP Internet access account.

Assuming that you have chosen an ISP and signed up for an Internet access account, we are now ready to configure the modem to connect via the ISP to the Internet using the built-in Windows 98 Internet services.

You will recall from Chapter Three, when we configured the NIC, that we first needed to install the NIC adapter driver, and then the network protocol (NetBEUI) that the NIC would be using to allow communication between NICs (and thus PCs) across the network.

In more or less the same way, in order to configure the modem to be able to communicate with the modem equipment at the ISP and thus to the Internet, we need first to install and configure a modem adapter driver, (which for Windows 98 is known as the 'Dial-Up Adapter'), and then to install and configure the network protocol (which in this case is TCP/IP). In fact you may also recall that we installed the TCP/IP protocol driver in Chapter Four when we installed the NetBEUI driver, and so will only now need to configure this to work with the Dial-Up Adapter.

These two setup procedures may appear rather technical, but once successfully set up, they will allow the day-to-day business of connecting to the Internet to proceed smoothly and easily and without having to be reconfigured, except perhaps if you choose to change your ISP.

Once we have set up the adapter and protocol settings, we will then need to set up the Windows 98 Dial-Up Networking utility. This utility simply manages the dial-up process itself, allowing you to enter different dial-up profiles for dialling into different services.

Dial-Up Adapter – Installation

You will first need to check that the 'Dial-Up Networking' facility was installed during the Windows 98 setup. From the Windows 98 Desktop view, double-click on 'My Computer' and check for the presence of 'Dial-Up Networking'. If this is not present, then you will need to install it from your Windows 98 CD or setup disks as follows:

1 Click on 'Start > Settings > Control Panel' to show the Control Panel.

2 Double-click on 'Add/Remove Programs' and then click on the 'Windows 98 Setup' tab.

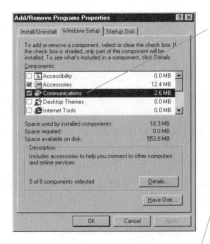

3 Double-click on 'Communications'.

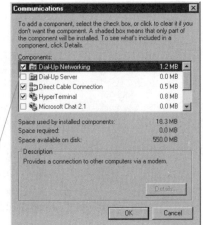

4 Select the 'Dial-Up Networking' box and click on 'OK'.

5 Click on 'OK' again and follow the usual instructions for loading the appropriate Windows 98 disk(s).

With 'Dial-Up Networking' present, install the 'Dial-Up Adapter' following the procedure opposite:

From the 'Control Panel' double-click on 'Network'.

From previous adapter/ protocol driver installations, the 'Network' window should look something like this:

2 Click on 'Add'.

3 Then select 'Adapter' and click 'Add'.

4 From the list of 'Manufacturers' select 'Microsoft' to reveal 'Dial-Up Adapter' and then click 'OK'.

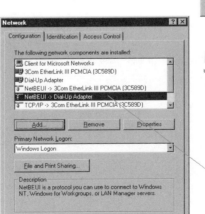

5 The 'Network' window will then show that the 'Dial-Up Adapter' and several protocols have been added. From the protocol drivers, the 'NetBEUI ->Dial-Up Adapter' can be safely removed by selecting it and clicking 'Remove'.

TCP/IP Services – Configuration

When you sign up with an ISP, you should be provided with the details of the various settings that you will need to configure your Windows 98 TCP/IP driver.

These may include the following:

- An IP address for your PC

- A 'Subnet Mask'

- The IP address of the 'Gateway'

- A 'Host' name, sometimes also called the 'username'

- A 'Domain' name

- The IP address(es) of the 'Domain Name Server'

You may need to call your ISP support line to get these details, which may be referred to in a slightly different manner, but these are the terms which Windows 98 uses for TCP/IP configuration. Some ISPs will dynamically allocate an IP address to each new connection. In this case some of the following settings will differ slightly, as explained in the steps.

To configure your TCP/IP driver, proceed as follows.

1 From the 'Control Panel' double-click on 'Network'.

2 From the list of installed network components, select the 'TCP/IP->Dial-Up Adapter'.

3 Click on 'Properties' and then click on 'OK' at the 'TCP/IP Properties Information' dialogue.

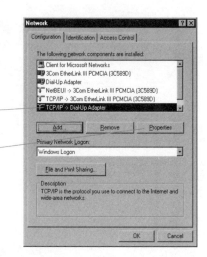

4 You will then be presented
with the 'TCP/IP Properties'
window. Select the 'IP
Address' tab at the top, if
this is not already selected.

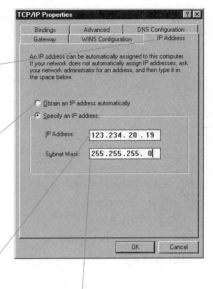

5 If your ISP allocates IP
addresses dynamically,
select 'Obtain IP address
automatically' and skip
steps 5 & 6. Otherwise
select the 'Specify an IP
Address' button.

6 Enter the 'IP Address' that
has been allocated to your
PC.

7 Enter the 'Subnet
Mask'(usually
255.255.255.0).

The details entered in the example above are for illustration
only.

To continue, select the
'Gateway' tab at the top of
the window.

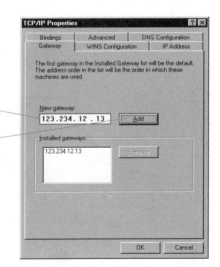

1 Enter the 'Gateway' IP
address.

2 Click 'Add'.

Modem Access – Configuration...cont'd

Next, select the 'DNS Configuration' tab.

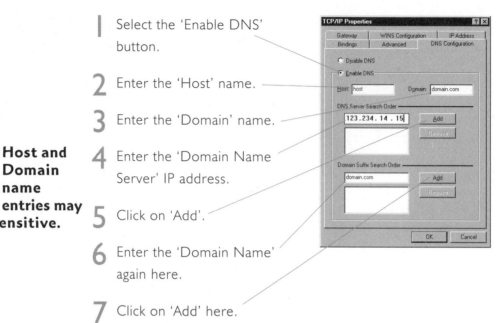

1   Select the 'Enable DNS' button.

2   Enter the 'Host' name.

3   Enter the 'Domain' name.

Host and Domain name entries may be case sensitive.

4   Enter the 'Domain Name Server' IP address.

5   Click on 'Add'.

6   Enter the 'Domain Name' again here.

7   Click on 'Add' here.

Now click on the 'Bindings' tab. From amongst the Bindings Settings (you may have more), check that the 'Client for Microsoft Networks' is ticked and the 'File and printer sharing for Microsoft Networks' is not.

1   Tick 'Client for Microsoft Networks'.

2   Un-tick 'File and printer sharing for Microsoft Networks'.

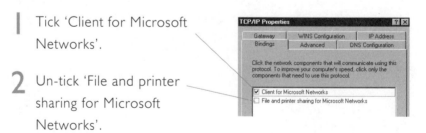

It is unlikely that you will need to set up the 'WINS Configuration' settings and can probably ignore this section except to check that the 'Disable WINS Resolution' setting is ticked.

Your ISP instructions should inform you if 'WIN Resolution' setting needs to be enabled, and if so, check with your ISP for details.

You can now click on the various tabs at the top of the 'TCP/IP Properties' window to check the various settings. Once you are happy that all of the above settings are correct, click on 'OK' at the bottom of whichever section you are in, and then click on 'OK' again at the bottom of the 'Network' window.

When you are prompted to restart Windows 98, click 'Yes' to save the TCP/IP settings.

Dial-Up Networking Configuration

Now that we have set up the adapter and protocol drivers, we need to define a 'Dial-Up Networking' connection profile for the ISP. This utility allows you to specify the local access telephone number as allocated by your ISP, and to set up the modem for that particular connection.

To configure this utility, proceed as follows:

You can Drag and Drop the 'My Computer' icon from the Desktop to the 'Start' button to create a short-cut from the 'Start' menu bar.

1 Minimise or close all of the current active Windows 98 windows until you are left with the Desktop view.

2 Double-click on 'My Computer'.

3 Double-click on 'Dial-Up Networking'.

4 Double-click on 'Make New Connection'. This will reveal the 'Make New Connection' wizard as follows.

5 Type over the 'My Connection' default with any text to describe your ISP connection profile (eg, 'ISP').

6 Your installed modem(s) will be displayed in the 'Select a modem' drop-down menu (my modem is displayed). If you have more than one modem installed, then select the one that you wish to use to connect to your ISP. Otherwise, click 'Next>'.

7 Enter the 'Area Code' and 'Telephone number' of your ISP access number.

8 Select the country in which you are located from the drop-down menu.

9 Click on 'Next >' and then 'Finish'. Your new connection profile will now be displayed in the 'Dial-Up Networking' window.

Having defined a new connection profile, we must now configure the modem and ISP server settings.

...cont'd

The modem settings required for your ISP connection may differ from those given below in some respects, but in most cases the settings given should work. If not, then consult your ISP for the appropriate modem settings.

Proceed as follows:

1   Right-click on the connection profile you have just created, and then click on 'Properties'.

2   Click on 'Configure'.

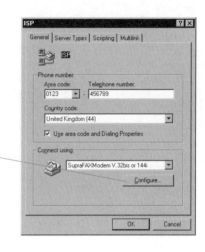

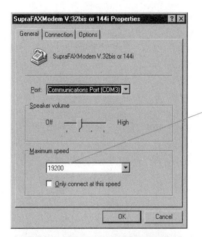

3   Check that the 'Maximum speed' setting is that which your modem will support, or if appropriate, as recommended by your ISP.

4   Click on the 'Connection' tab.

5   Check that the modem settings are as indicated, or set according to your ISP.

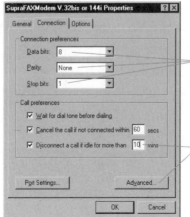

6   Activate the 'Disconnect a call if idle...' tick-box and set an appropriate time. Then click on 'Advanced'.

Modem Access – Configuration...cont'd

7 If your modem will support 'Error control' and 'Compression' (most likely) then ensure that the 'Use error control' tick-box is activated, along with the 'Compress data' tick-box.

8 Ensure that 'Use flow control' is activated. If using an internal modem, then select 'Hardware (RTS/CTS)'. If you are using an external modem, then you may need to select 'Software (XON/XOFF)'.

9 If 'Modulation type' is required (not required in this case), select 'Standard'. Click on 'OK'.

You will be returned to the 'Modem Properties' window. Now click on the 'Options' tab.

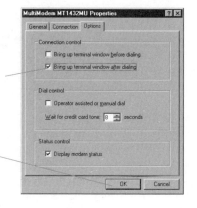

I Activate the 'Bring up terminal window after dialling' tick-box.

2 Click on 'OK'.

Finally, we need to configure the 'Server Type' settings.

...cont'd

1 From the 'Properties' window as in the previous Step 2, click on 'Server Types'.

2 Select 'PPP: Internet, Windows NT Server,Windows 98...' from the drop-down menu.

3 Ensure that the only box ticked is 'TCP/IP'.

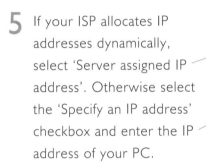

4 Click on 'TCP/IP Settings...'.

5 If your ISP allocates IP addresses dynamically, select 'Server assigned IP address'. Otherwise select the 'Specify an IP address' checkbox and enter the IP address of your PC.

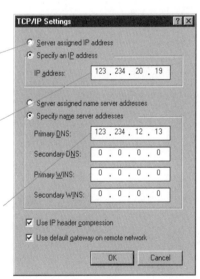

 In some cases the 'DNS Server' will also be assigned automatically by the ISP.

6 Activate the 'Specify name server addresses' checkbox and enter the IP address(es) of the Domain Name Server (DNS) in the Primary DNS location, and the Secondary DNS if appropriate.

7 Leave the 'Use IP header compression' and 'Use default gateway on remote network' ticked, and click on 'OK' in the 'TCP/IP Setting', 'Server Types' and the main 'Properties' window.

Modem Access – Connecting

Now that we have completed the somewhat laborious process of setting up your modem Internet access, you should now be able to successfully connect to the Internet.

What we have set up so far is in fact the 'manual' method of connecting to the Internet via an ISP, and we will now look at connecting using this method. Once this is successful, we will then look at how to automate the process.

To connect to your ISP manually, you will need your 'Host' account name and password as well as your IP address.

Manual Dial-Up

We will use this procedure to test your Internet access before proceeding to the automatic dial-up configuration.

Your ISP will have supplied you with a 'username' which may well be the same as your 'Host' name, and a 'password' to allow access to your Internet account. You will also need your IP address.

Proceed as follows:

From the 'Dial-Up Networking' window, double-click on the connection profile that you have just created. This will start the 'Connect To' window as follows:

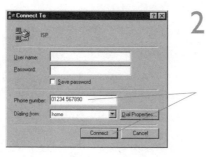

2 Check that the dial-up number to your ISP is correct and, ignoring any 'Username' or 'Password' entries that may appear, click on 'Connect'.

The following will appear while the modem dials the number:

...cont'd

Once connected, a window similar to the following should appear, requesting a 'username' or 'host' input. The exact text may differ for different ISPs. If it does not appear, or if the output text is garbled, you may need to examine or reset your modem settings.

3 Enter your 'username' being careful to use the correct type case (Capitalisation or lower-case) and press the 'Enter' key.

 Make a note of the exact text that appears as the command prompt. You may need this later.

4 You will then be prompted to enter a 'password'. Type this in (for security reasons it may not appear on screen, so type carefully!) and press 'Enter'. If this is accepted, then a command prompt will appear (see HOT TIP).

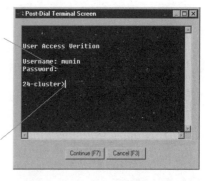

5 At the command prompt, type 'ppp', then a space, and then your IP address. Again, type this carefully as any mistakes are unlikely to be correctable, except by starting the dial-up process from scratch.

6 Press the 'Enter' key. You should now see a response from the ISP giving details of your PPP connection, followed by a string of garbled characters. When this occurs, click on 'Continue' or press the 'F7' key.

You should now see this...

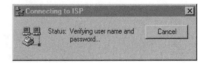

...followed after a short delay by a 'Logging on' dialogue, and then a 'Connection Established' window. If so . . . Congratulations! You are now connected to the Internet! Disconnect by clicking on the 'connected' icon in the Windows 98 control bar, and then clicking on 'Disconnect'.

Automatic Dial-Up

Having established that your Internet dial-up connection is working correctly, we can now automate the process so that your 'username', 'password' and IP address are passed to the ISP server without you having to type then in every time.

> **Sample Dial-Up Scripts can be found in the 'Program Files > Accessories' directory as 'xxx.scp'.**

This is done by defining a 'Dial-Up Script', which is simply a set of text containing these parameters, and which is processed when you initiate the modem dial-up. Your ISP may be able to supply you with a script file that will be suitable for your particular type of connection.

If your ISP can supply you with a suitable script (this will be a file with an '.scp' suffix), then copy it now into the C:/ Program Files/Accessories' directory (or equivalent if your Windows 98 system is installed elsewhere). If not, then you will need to edit your own script. The script outlined below is intended as a guide only, and may not work for your particular ISP without further modification. To produce this sample script, proceed as follows:

1 Click on 'Start > Programs > Accessories', then click on 'Notepad'. This will open the simple Windows 98 text editor with a blank page.

2 Copy out the following text, using the tab keys where necessary so that the text is laid out as shown. Insert your own 'username', 'password', and IP address as indicated.

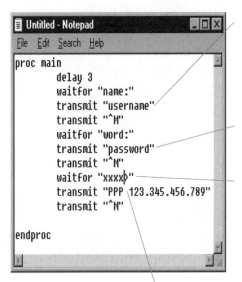

Replace 'username' with your own username. Do not omit the quotation marks.

Replace 'password' with your own password.

Replace the 'xxxx>' with exactly the text that appeared as the 'command prompt' when you used the manual dial-up method.

Replace the '123.345.456.789' with your own IP address. Do not omit the 'PPP ' (remember the space) or the quotation marks.

3 When completed, click on 'File' and 'Save As' and save the file as 'isp.scp' in the 'C:/Program Files/Accessories/' directory as above.

Modem Access – Connecting...cont'd

To install your script, proceed as follows:

1 From the 'Desktop' view (ie, minimize all current windows), double-click on 'My Computer'. Then double-click on 'Dial-Up Networking'.

2 Right-click on the ISP connection profile that you created in 'Dial-Up Networking Configuration', and then click on 'Properties'. This will bring up the 'General' properties of this connection profile as follows:

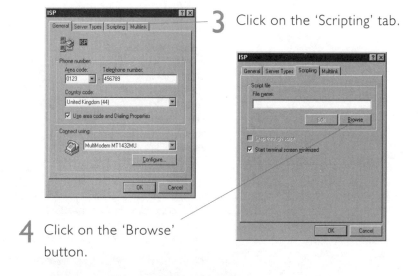

3 Click on the 'Scripting' tab.

4 Click on the 'Browse' button.

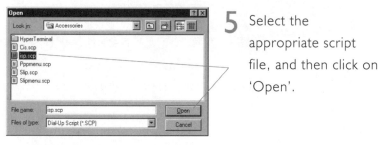

5 Select the appropriate script file, and then click on 'Open'.

6 The script file and path now appears in the 'File name' entry. Click on 'OK'.

Adjusting Modem Properties

Before we can use the script for automatic dial-up, however, we need to make an adjustment to the 'Modem Properties' as follows:

1. Right-click on the ISP connection profile that you created in 'Dial-Up Networking Configuration', and then click on 'Properties'. This will bring up the 'General' properties of this connection profile:

2. Click on 'Configure' to bring up the modem properties window, and select the 'Options' tag.

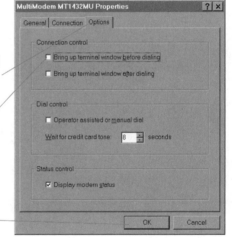

3. De-select the 'Bring up terminal window after dialling' option, and click 'OK'.

4. Click on 'OK' again in the general properties window.

Now if you double-click on your ISP connection profile icon or listing item, the connection process to your ISP should be automated. If you have problems, then you may need to contact your ISP to check the scripting details.

Creating an ISP Connection Short-Cut

To make access to your Internet connection profile easily available from within any application, you can make a short-cut to the 'Start' menu as follows:

1 Close or minimise all open Windows 98 to get the 'Desktop' view.

2 Double-click on 'My Computer' and then double-click 'Dial-Up Networking'.

3 Select the connection profile that you recently created for your ISP connection, and then drag-and-drop it to the 'Start' button at the bottom left of the screen.

You will now find that an icon for the profile exists in the 'Start' menu, allowing you easy access to the Internet in just a few clicks.

Troubleshooting

If you find that you are not able to connect to your ISP, it may be that your Access Mode within Windows 98 is not set for modem access. To resolve this, follow the instructions in the last section of this chapter, 'Switching Between Access Modes'(page 146).

Sharing a Fax Modem

In the same way that it is possible to share printer and directory/file resources over a network, it is also possible to share a fax modem that is installed on one of the networked PCs. This facility is not, however, a standard part of the Windows 98 system setup and requires the installation of some specialised files from the Windows 98 CD.

 Make sure that you have installed and tested a Fax Modem on one of the networked PCs before attempting to configure the fax sharing service.

The specific files required will depend on your existing Windows 98 setup. To setup fax sharing you will certainly need to install a fax enabling file from the Windows 98 CD. If you do not have either Windows Messaging, Microsoft Exchange client, or Microsoft Outlook (all MAPI clients) installed on the PCs that will need access to the shared fax service, you will also need to install the Windows Messaging installation file onto each PC **before** installing the fax enabling file.

In outlining the fax sharing configuration, I will assume that you have none of the above installed. If you do have any of the three programs mentioned above installed, then you can skip the next section.

Installing Windows Messaging

1   Insert the Windows 98 CD, double-click on the 'tools/oldwin95/message/intl/wms.exe' file, and click 'Yes' to 'Are you sure....' and then 'Yes' again.

2   Select 'Yes' to the question 'Have you used Windows Messaging before' (trust me!). Click 'Next>'.

3   De-select the 'Microsoft Mail' entry and then select the 'Manually configure information services' option. Click 'Next>'.

4   Enter 'Fax' into the Profile Name dialogue. Click 'Next>' and then 'OK' in the 'Fax Properties' window.

5   Click on 'Finish'.

Sharing a Fax Modem...cont'd

Installing the Fax enabling software

1. Insert the Windows 98 CD, double-click on the 'tools/oldwin95/message/intl/awfax.exe' file, and then click 'Yes' (provided you are sure that the conditions are fulfilled).

2. Click on 'Yes' to restart your computer.

Once you have installed both the fax enabling software and at least one of the above MAPI clients onto each of the PCs that will be sharing the fax service (including the PC that actually has the fax modem installed), you will then configure the MAPI clients as follows.

In much the same way that shared resources were configured in Chapter 4, the PC that has the fax modem installed will be configured to make the shared fax resource available over the network, and the PCs that will need to use the fax resource will be configured to access it over the network.

Making the Fax Modem available......

If you already had a suitable MAPI client installed, then you will need to create a new 'Profile' called 'Fax' and install only the 'Microsoft Fax' service.

1. On the fax modem PC, start the MAPI client (Windows Messaging/Inbox or Outlook, etc) from the desktop, and select the 'Fax' profile that we created earlier. Click on 'OK'.

2. Click on 'Tools > Services' from the toolbar.

3. Click on 'Add', select 'Microsoft Fax' from the options and click on 'OK'.

4. You will be asked to specify certain details....click on 'Yes', and enter your return 'Fax number' as a minimum. Click on 'OK'.

5. Click on 'Yes' to specify a fax modem. Select the 'Let other people......' option, and click on 'OK' to select the default hard drive.

...cont'd

 If you intend to use the fax modem PC to source faxes, then you may need to install the 'Personal Address Book' by 'Adding' it as a service in the same manner as with the 'Microsoft Fax' service.

6 If you only have one fax modem installed, then this will already be selected. Otherwise, choose from the list. Click on 'OK', 'OK' again and 'OK' once more to finish the configuration. Now restart the MAPI client and leave it running.

Configuring shared fax resource access......

1 From the PCs requiring the shared fax access, start the MAPI client (Windows Messaging/Inbox or Outlook, etc) from the desktop, and click on 'New' in the 'Choose a Profile' window.

2 Select only the 'Microsoft Fax' service, de-selecting any other options, and click on 'Next>'.

3 Enter 'Fax' as the 'Profile Name' and click on 'Next>'.

4 Click on 'Add' as if to add a new fax modem, select 'Network fax server' and click on 'OK'.

 If the '\\host\fax\' is not accepted, try closing the MAPI client on the Fax Modem PC and restarting it.

5 Enter the 'Path' in the form '\\host\fax' where 'host' is the name of the PC that has the shared fax resource. Then select this new entry and click on 'Next>'.

6 Fill out the name and fax number details as required and click on 'Next>'.

7 Replace 'mailbox.pab' with 'fax.pab' and click on 'Next>', then replace 'mailbox.pst' with 'fax.pst' (see BEWARE) and click on 'Next>'. Click on 'Finish', then 'OK', and then restart the PC.

 To carry out Step 7 is especially important if you already have a MAPI client installed, as leaving the default file locations can overwrite existing files.

You should now be able to send documents from your Microsoft word processing programs to the shared fax resource by 'File > Print'-ing them, selecting the 'Microsoft Fax' option as the printer (drop-down menu button in the Printer > Name dialogue), and choosing the 'Fax' profile . Enter a name and fax number, click on 'Add to List > Next > Next > Next > Finish' and off it goes......!

ISDN Access – Configuration

In Chapter Six, we looked at setting up two types of ISDN Router.

We now need to set up the Windows 98 network protocol drivers and IP address configuration to allow the network PCs to establish ISDN Internet access across the network, via the router.

Whilst both types of router are capable of being set up in a number of different ways, the pre-configured router (as supplied by Demon) is set up to enable specific method of using the allocated IP addresses. We will first look at the Windows 98 that is compatible with this method.

By way of contrast, the 3Com router can be set up to use an alternative method of allocating IP addresses. Instead of using a range of ISP specified IP addresses, this method will allow the networked PCs to access the Internet via a single ISP specified IP address.

The advantage of using this method is that an ISDN account using a single IP address can often be a more cost effective way of allowing networked PCs to access the Internet. Not all ISPs however will allow this kind of access, and those that do will often place restrictions on the type of access allowed by this method. With Demon, the difference is that a multiple IP address account is given a dedicated ISDN dial-in number at the ISP end, whereas the single IP address account shares a dial-in number with several other users.

We will shortly look at both types of setup, but first we will briefly examine the new situation with regard to the protocol drivers that we will need when accessing the Internet via an ISDN link.

In Chapter Four, we not only installed the NetBEUI protocol drivers necessary for running the Windows 98 network, we also installed the TCP/IP protocol. It is this protocol which allows us to communicate with the Internet.

If you have previously used a modem to communicate with the Internet, then you will have installed the 'Dial-Up Adapter' as described earlier in this chapter.

When using an ISDN Router, we no longer need to use the 'Dial-Up Adapter' that we may have used for modem access. The first thing to do therefore is to remove the 'Dial-Up Adapter' if present, leaving only the TCP/IP and NetBEUI drivers in place.

To examine the current state of your network drivers, and remove any that we no longer need, proceed as follows:

1 Open the Control Panel, and double-click 'Network' as before to open the Network configuration window. Your network configuration panel may look something like this.

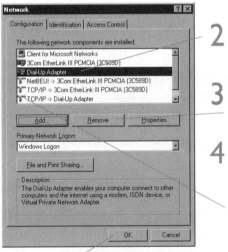

2 To remove the 'Dial-Up Adapter' driver, select it...

3 ...and then click on 'Remove'.

4 You can also select and remove the 'TCP/IP driver that is associated with the 'Dial-Up Adapter.

5 Once all of the drivers that are no longer required have been removed, click on OK. Restart Windows 98 when prompted to do so.

Multiple IP Address Setup

This type of configuration should be used in association with the pre-configured router as supplied by Demon.

We will outline a single networked PC configuration, and then describe how subsequent PCs will differ.

Our example IP addresses range from 195.11.192.2 to 195.11.192.6 (ie, four addresses for four PCs). The Demon router will already have been pre-configured as 195.11.192.1. (or similar) making five ISP assigned IP addresses in total. You may have any number of ISP assigned IP addresses, but the first will always be assigned to the router. The router IP address then becomes the 'Gateway' address to the Internet.

We will be assigning sequential IP addresses, one to each networked PC, so begin by selecting the PC that you wish to assign the first IP address value to, and configure this PC as follows:

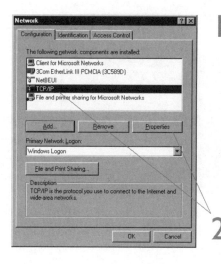

1 From within Windows 98, bring up the 'Network' configuration panel as before (ie, by clicking on 'Start > Settings > Control Panel'), then double-click on 'Network' and select the 'Configuration' tab.

2 Select the 'TCP/IP' entry, and Click on 'Properties'.

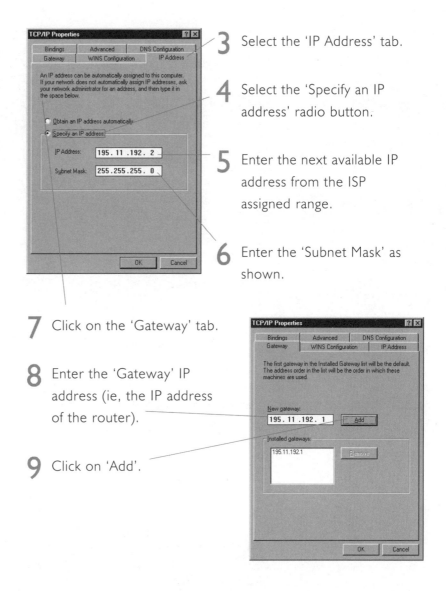

3 Select the 'IP Address' tab.

4 Select the 'Specify an IP address' radio button.

5 Enter the next available IP address from the ISP assigned range.

6 Enter the 'Subnet Mask' as shown.

7 Click on the 'Gateway' tab.

8 Enter the 'Gateway' IP address (ie, the IP address of the router).

9 Click on 'Add'.

Thus far we have configured this PC's IP address, and defined a path to the 'Gateway' router. We now need to define the path to the DNS server, usually located at the ISP site. To do this, we continue the TCP/IP setup as follows:

1 Select the 'DNS Configuration' tab.

2 Select the 'Enable DNS' radio button.

3 Enter the 'Host' and 'Domain' names as shown.

4 Enter the IP address of the DNS as supplied by Demon, and click 'Add'. Repeat this process if more than one DNS is available.

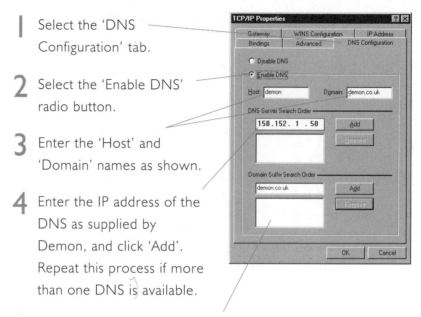

5 Enter the 'Domain Suffix Search Order' as shown, and click 'Add'.

6 Click on 'OK', and then on 'OK' in the 'Network' window. Restart Windows 98 when prompted to do so.

We have now configured the first PC on the network. For the rest of the PCs, follow exactly the same procedure, with the exception of the IP address. For each subsequent PC, the IP address will be the next available IP address from the range of ISP specified addresses – eg, the next IP address in our range will be 195.11.192.3, and is entered in the IP Address section of the TCP/IP Configuration window as follows:

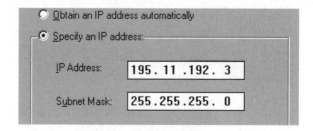

...cont'd

Having configured your network PCs with suitable IP addresses, you should now be able to connect to the Internet via your Demon router, provided the PC is connected to the router via the network, and the router is connected to the ISDN line.

If you experience any problems with the Demon router setup, you can call Demon support on 0181 371 1010.

Single IP Address Setup

This setup procedure is suitable in association with the 3Com Office Connect 510 ISDN Router, and is specified here as an alternative to the Demon pre-configured router option when connecting to the appropriate Demon ISDN account. It may not be suitable when connecting other routers to other ISP ISDN accounts.

The single IP address method uses a feature of the 3Com router known as Network Address Translation. This was set up previously on the 3Com router when we configured it in Chapter Six. We now need to set up the Windows 98 TCP/IP drivers on our networked PCs to use this facility.

 Other routers that support 'Network Address Translation' can also be configured in this way.

During the 3Com router setup procedure, we assigned the IP address 20.0.0.1 to the router. This address now becomes the 'Gateway' IP address for our network. We can now assign any address in the range 20.0.0.2 to 20.0.0.255 to our networked PCs. This means that we can have up to 253 networked PCs attached to the networked ISDN connection.

To configure the Windows 98 TCP/IP driver in this way, simply follow the same procedure as for configuring for a multiple IP address setup, but when you come to configuring the 'Gateway' IP address, enter 20.0.0.1. This applies to all of the networked PC configurations. When you come to configuring the IP address setting for each PC, enter any IP address from the range 20.0.0.2 to 20.0.0.255. The examples overleaf should help you.

ISDN Access – Configuration...cont'd

Having chosen your first networked PC, and from within Windows 98 opened the 'Network' configuration window and selected the 'Properties' for the TCP/IP driver, proceed as follows:

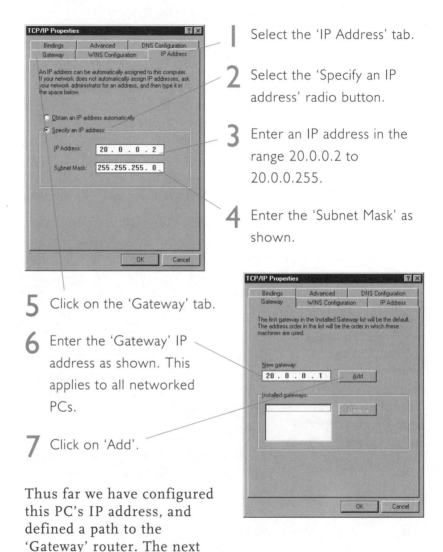

1 Select the 'IP Address' tab.

2 Select the 'Specify an IP address' radio button.

3 Enter an IP address in the range 20.0.0.2 to 20.0.0.255.

4 Enter the 'Subnet Mask' as shown.

5 Click on the 'Gateway' tab.

6 Enter the 'Gateway' IP address as shown. This applies to all networked PCs.

7 Click on 'Add'.

Thus far we have configured this PC's IP address, and defined a path to the 'Gateway' router. The next step is to define the IP address(es) of the DNS server. Do this by following the same procedure as for the multiple IP address setup. Finally, complete the TCP/IP driver configuration as follows:

8 Click on 'OK', and then on 'OK' in the 'Network' window. Restart Windows 98 when prompted to do so.

We have now configured the first PC on the network. For the rest of the PCs, follow the same procedure with the exception of the IP address entry. For each subsequent PC, the IP address will be the next available IP address from the range 20.0.0.2 to 20.0.0.255. For example, the next IP address in our range will be 20.0.0.3, and will be entered in the IP Address section of the TCP/IP Configuration window as follows:

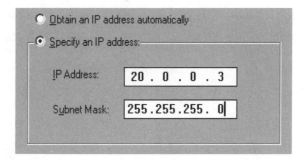

Having configured your network PCs with a suitable IP addresses, you should now be able to connect to the Internet via your 3Com router, provided the PC is connected to the router via the network, and the router is connected to the ISDN line.

If you experience any problems with the 3Com router setup, you can call 3Com support on 0800 966197.

Troubleshooting

If you find that you are not able to connect to your ISP, it may be that your Access Mode within Windows 98 is not set for network access. To resolve this follow the instructions in the next section of this chapter, 'Switching Between Access Modes'.

Switching Between Access Modes

The Access Mode is an arbitrary term that I have chosen to describe the state of a switch within Windows 98 which determines whether the TCP/IP driver refers to a modem connection or to a network connection for Internet access.

This switch is accessible by running through the 'Connection Wizard'. This utility is available via 'Start > Programs > Internet Explorer' if you have installed Internet Explorer.

To switch between modes, find and start the 'Connection Wizard' and run through the setup as follows:

I Select 'I have an existing Internet account...' from the first window, and click on 'Next>'.

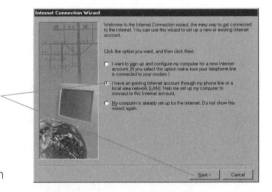

2 Click on 'Next>' in the following window.

3 Select the appropriate 'Access Mode' for your requirements. Click on 'Next>'.

4 Click on 'Next>' in the following window, and then 'Finish'. You may then need to reboot your computer for the new settings to take effect.

Using the Internet

In this chapter, we will look at some of the Internet's various applications, and describe some of the more popular software packages and utilities available to make use of its many facilities.

Covers

Chapter Eight

Using the Internet – Overview

Once you have gained access to the Internet, you will want to begin using the enormous capabilities that it can offer as soon as possible.

There are a host of software packages and utilities available to allow you to do this, each with its own specific capabilities and peculiarities.

Before we look at some of these packages, we will take a look at some of the various facilities that the Internet can provide.

Think of the Internet simply as a means to an end, providing the communication medium across which a number of alternative types of communication are possible.

By far the most popular uses that the Internet can be put to are:

- 'Browsing' Web Sites

- Sending and Receiving E-mail

- Reading and posting to Newsgroups

Web Sites

Web sites are essentially a collection of specialised files called web pages that are located remotely on a web 'server'.

These files are constructed according to a standard that allows any web 'browser' to be able to interpret and present the information contained within.

This is the specific job of the 'browser' – to load the web pages using an Internet connection, and then to interpret the contents of these pages so that the information contained within is presented and laid out in a manner specified by the web page coding.

The information contained can be simple text, text with images, or include multimedia content such as animations, video clips and sound clips. It can even effectively be an interactive program that responds to user input.

This is the ideal. In practice however, the 'standards' are constantly in development and so a web page made for today's 'standards' may not be best presented by an older browser.

One of the most powerful features of these specialised web page files is the ability to embed 'links' within them. The 'links' are contained within the text or images or other elements of the web page, and effectively direct the browser to load another specified web page. This page is addressed using a standard addressing system, so that the appropriate page can be located and loaded.

The standard addressing systems means that the files to be loaded can be located on any other web server, literally anywhere in the world. Thus a single web site can span a number of different 'server' sites across the world.

The ability of a web page to contain links means that it is possible to build vast hierarchies of web pages, linking relevant pieces of information together.

E-mail
The Internet is most often used to send and receive e-mail.

E-mail is again a specialised type of file transfer using the Internet TCP/IP protocol as the communication medium. The E-mail is sent from the PC to a specialised remote e-mail 'server'. The e-mail is then directed by the e-mail server over the Internet to other e-mail servers using a standard e-mail addressing system, en-route to its final destination where it is delivered to the destination PC.

The Internet e-mail system is not to be confused with other types of 'proprietary' e-mail systems commonly used to relay messages internally within many large organisations.

E-mail normally contains simple text messages, but files can also be 'attached' to the e-mail and sent together with the text. Thus you might send an entire word processor document as an attachment to a simple e-mail describing its function and contents.

The 'attachment' can then be opened using a suitable word processing application at the receiver end complete with all of its inherent layout properties, etc. This capability can be used to send any type of file as an attachment to an e-mail.

All e-mail contains essential information about the e-mail transfer process in the e-mail 'header'. This information records the destination and sender address as well as other information concerning the timing and route taken by the e-mail. The header is not normally visible within an e-mail, but can be viewed if required.

The address details are especially useful as they allow responses to e-mail to be automatically addressed to the original sender.

Other standard options allow received e-mail to be forwarded to another recipient, or e-mail to be copied to several recipients at once.

Newsgroups

Across the Internet are maintained many 'newsgroups'. Newsgroups are essentially a specialised form of e-mail facility where messages can be posted and viewed by anyone who is 'joined' to the newsgroup, rather than being restricted to a specified recipient as with e-mail. Thus members of a newsgroup can share and discuss information concerning a particular subject that the newsgroup is concerned with.

Many more specialised Newsgroup browsing software packages are available. Try browsing some of the many 'Shareware' sites to locate these.

Again, newsgroup 'servers' are used to supply this facility. A newsgroup is named and dedicated to a particular subject. An Internet user can then connect to a newsgroup server and 'join' any of the listed newsgroups.

Messages are 'posted' into this area by anyone who is a member of the newsgroup. All posted messages are then visible to all other members of the newsgroup.

Any member can then comment on a message. Several comments on a particular subject then form what is known as a 'thread'. The question and answer process within a thread can go on for many messages and for some time, depending on the interest raised by the subject of the thread.

In this way a conversation between members of a newsgroup can be maintained. It's a bit like being a member of a hobby club. Many Internet users use these newsgroups to stay ahead of current developments within a specialised area.

The information contained within a newsgroup often remains on the newsgroup server for some time, and is then frequently searchable. In this way it is possible to see if a particular enquiry has been covered before, and then read the relevant sections, rather than going through the process all over again.

Newsgroups can be a mixed blessing. Whenever you connect to a newsgroup server, all of the messages from all over the world within the newsgroup will be downloaded onto your machine, whether or not these are relevant to you. You then need to browse through all of the messages to see if anything interesting has cropped up. This can take up a lot of time on a busy newsgroup, not to mention the line time taken to download all of these messages.

There are several mechanisms available to ease this situation. Newsgroups are often divided into 'topics' so that you can restrict your membership to only those topics of interest within a more generalised newsgroup.

Many newsgroup browsers will allow you to only download the subject headings of the messages, so that you can decide to download the complete messages later if they seem relevant.

Web Browser – Internet Explorer

 Netscape Navigator and other web browser software can often be obtained from the cover CDs of many PC magazines.

There are many web browsers available, but by far the most popular are those from Microsoft and from Netscape.

The Microsoft web browser is called the Internet Explorer (IE) and is fully integrated with Windows 98. As such, we will concern ourselves here with the configuration and operation of the Internet Explorer web browser. The range of configuration options available within IE is fairly extensive, so we will only be looking at the basic settings that you will need to familiarise yourself with the essential elements.

Getting Started

There are three ways to start up IE.

The simplest way is to click on the blue 'e' on the Windows 98 Control Bar, just next to the 'Start' button.

The second method is to click on the blue 'e' on the desktop. The third is to click on 'Start > Programs > Internet Explorer'.

When IE starts up, you may find that the system prompts you to initiate a dial-up connection. This is because the default setting for IE is to go straight to a Microsoft web site, and so it attempts to do this by connecting. For the time being simply cancel the dial-up dialogue or click on 'Stay Offline'.

Once IE is running, the controls at the top of the page will look something like those opposite. We will examine each Tool Bar individually.

The Tool Bars

Menu Bar   Standard Buttons

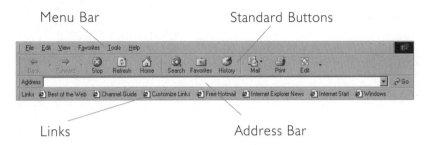

Links   Address Bar

Internet Explorer 5 screens are used in this book – there may be some differences if you have another version.

Links

The 'Links' are a handy set of quick short-cuts provided by Microsoft to some useful web sites. You can click on any of these as an easy way of getting going on the World Wide Web.

Address Bar

The 'Address Bar' is the area where the web address of the web site you are currently connected is displayed. This will generally be in the form 'http://www.etc.etc'. This is also the area where you can enter the web address of the site that you want to go to.

Type in the address (you do not need to include the 'http://' bit; just start with 'www...etc') and press enter, and you will then be connected to the web site at that address, provided of course that you are connected to the Internet in the first place.

Standard Buttons

The 'Standard Buttons' are the basic navigation tools that you will frequently use when browsing the Internet. As well as the buttons that allow you to move backwards and forwards within a web site, IE also provides a range of other tools to enhance your browsing. The following descriptions include reference to various IE settings which will be covered later:

The 'Back' button is used to return to the previous web page. Clicking on the small down arrow to the right of the main 'back' arrow will display a 'clickable' list of the pages that have previously been visited, allowing you to jump back more than one page at a time.

The 'Forward' button is used in a similar fashion, to go to the following page within a web site. Of course, you must have previously visited this 'following' page and gone 'back' from it in order to return 'forwards'. Again, the small down button presents a clickable list of following pages.

The 'Stop' button does just as it suggests. When a web page begins to load, it will continue to do so until all of the content is loaded, regardless of how long this might take. If a page is loading and you decide that you want to stop and do something else instead, then clicking on the 'Stop' button will stop the current page from loading fully.

The 'Refresh' button again does just as it suggests. If for some reason a page fails to load correctly, then clicking the refresh button will reload the page and probably thus correct the problem. It can also be useful if the page gets 'stuck' as a result of an Internet bottleneck. Clicking on refresh will often recall the page via a different, less congested route.

...cont'd

The 'Home' button is used to get to a predetermined web page. This button can be set to point to a particular web address, so that when you click on it you go straight to that page. This can either be a page on the Internet (eg, your favourite search engine), or a more local page either on your PC or on the local network (eg, to a page containing a list of your favourite web sites). This is also the page that will be loaded when you start IE.

The 'Search' button reveals a list alongside the main display area of some of the more popular Search Engines that are available on the Internet, together with a text input box that allows you to enter a keyword to search on. Clicking on the Search button again removes this list from the display.

The 'Favorites' button reveals a clickable list of your favourite web sites. Initially this list is supplied by Microsoft, but it is highly configurable to allow you to add and organise your own list. Again, clicking on the button a second time removes the display.

The 'History' button reveals a clickable list of web sites and pages that you have recently visited. The number of days previous that visited sites are recorded is configurable. A second click reverses this.

Web Browser – Internet Explorer...cont'd

The 'Mail' button allows you to send an e-mail from within IE. Clicking it opens whichever e-mail package that is specified under the IE setup.

The 'Print' button simply sends the current web page to a printer. Printer configuration options are specified under the Printer Setup.

The 'Edit' button allows you to edit the current web page. Clicking on this button will send a copy of the current web page to the default text editor. This allows you to view and edit the contents which can then be saved on your local PC, or to the web site's host location if you have access.

Menu Bar

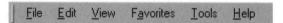

From the Menu Bar, you can access all of the web browser settings by means of drop down menus. We will briefly examine each in turn, and look in detail only at the most important configuration options.

...cont'd

File Menu

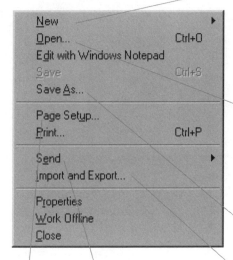

Options to open a new web browser, send an e-mail message or newsgroup posting, and add an entry to the address book.

Open a new web page, either by browsing files from a local PC, or from a remote web site by entering its web address.

Save a web page as a file to the local system.

Options to send the current web page, either as an e-mail, or to the Desktop as a shortcut.

Start an Import/Export wizard, which will allow you to import your Favourites and Cookie settings from other browsers.

Options to control the way that the web page is printed

Preview of the printed page layout.

Paper size options.

Options to code for various items to be placed in the Header and Footer of the printed page. See the Help file under 'print settings' for details of the available codes.

Click here to select which of the available printers to print to.

Web Browser – Internet Explorer...cont'd

Edit Menu

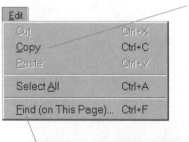

Copy parts of the current web page to the 'Clipboard' by marking them using the mouse and then clicking on 'Copy'.

A very useful feature that allows you to search the contents of the current web page for text as specified in the input area.

View Menu

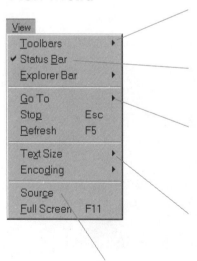

Options to hide or display all of the various types of Toolbar.

Hide or display the 'Status Bar' at the bottom of the display area.

Displays recent browsing history, and allows you to 'go to' the history items directly.

Increase or decrease the size of the default browser font setting.

View the HTML coding for the current web page. Mainly useful to web page developers.

...cont'd

Favorites Menu

The 'Favorites' menu is a function that allows you to store the web address of your favourite web sites in an efficient and easily accessible way, so that you can return to them without having to search. You can arrange individual web site address so that they fall into suitable categories that you can create in the form of folders.

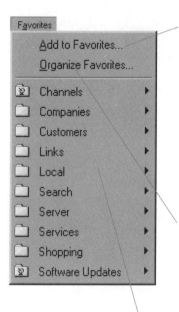

When you have found a web page that you want to save, click here to save it to your 'Favorites' listing. From the next window you can enter a name for the page reference, and use the 'Create in >>' button to either select an existing folder that you wish to save it in, or to create a new folder.

Use the 'Organise Favorites' feature to move the listings from one folder to another, to delete a listing, or to rename.

Some example 'Favorites' folders.

Web Browser – Internet Explorer...cont'd

Tools

Allows access to various browser tools, as well as the browser settings.

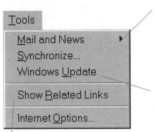

Access to the Mail and Newsgroup programs as defined in the 'Programs Tab' (see Internet Options).

Direct link to the Microsoft Windows Update website.

A powerful new feature which searches a database for websites that are related to the site currently being displayed.

Internet Options

From here you can access most of the major settings for configuring the IE browser.

General Tab

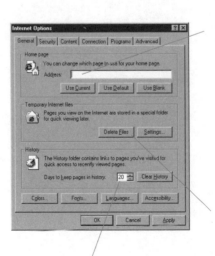

Enter the default web page that IE will load on start-up and when the 'Home' icon is selected from the 'Standard Toolbar'.

IE stores details of previously visited web pages in the 'Temporary Internet files' directory. Use the 'Delete Files' button to clear these.

Set the number of days worth of previously visited web pages here. The 'Clear History' button will clear these entries.

Security Tab

When you access a web site, the information that is passed between the web server and your PC's browser is available to many intermediate Internet systems. This means there is a *possibility* that any confidential information you might enter (eg, credit card numbers) *may* be available to 'persons of ill intent'. In reality, the likelihood of this occurring is limited, but IE provides a service that allows you to assign different levels of security to different web sites. It does this by dividing the sites that you can access into four categories called 'Zones', and then allows you to choose from four security levels for each category. Each security level is associated with a series of security checks that can be provided by various 'Internet Explorer aware' web site servers.

The addresses of web sites that support this kind of security system can then be added to one of the four categories, so that the security service level associated with that category is applied wherever you access that particular web site.

The default 'Zone' that is applied to all sites of unknown security status is 'Internet' and this has the default security status set to 'Medium'. Other 'Zones' include 'Local intranet' for locally available web sites (default Medium), 'Trusted sites' for web sites that support the security system (default Low), and 'Restricted sites' for those web sites suspected of having dubious security (default High).

Expert users can define their own security level configuration by using the 'Custom' option, and then selecting the 'Setting' button. This presents a list of all of the available security options, each of which is associated with a particular action or security function that is implemented or not when a web site is accessed.

Web Browser – Internet Explorer...cont'd

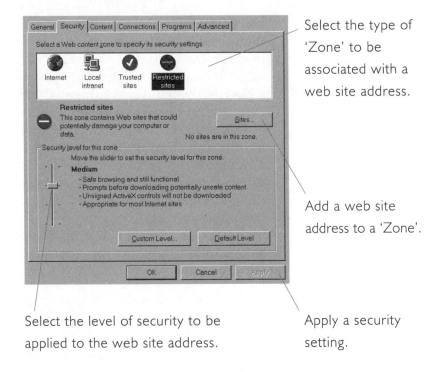

Select the type of 'Zone' to be associated with a web site address.

Add a web site address to a 'Zone'.

Select the level of security to be applied to the web site address.

Apply a security setting.

Content Tab

Certain web sites on the Internet use a system of 'content ratings' that can inform the IE web browser of the kind of content that the web site contains. This allows you to select which type of content may, or may not, be viewed by a particular IE user according to these ratings, with the 'user' being identified as part of the Windows 98 system settings. Thus, if a web site rating indicates that the content might be of an adult or offensive nature, and therefore not suitable for children (for example), the IE browser can detect this, and prevent this site from being accessed by a specific user.

The settings for this service are fairly involved, and we will not cover them here. Suffice to say that if you choose to enable this facility, it may limit the defined user to only those sites that support this facility.

Connection Tab

The Connection tab allows a series of settings to determine how you connect to the Internet.

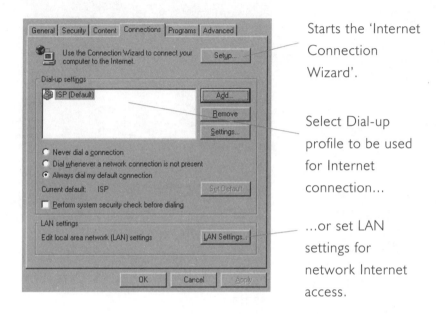

Starts the 'Internet Connection Wizard'.

Select Dial-up profile to be used for Internet connection...

...or set LAN settings for network Internet access.

Programs Tab

From here you are able to select which programs are used by the browser to edit web pages, send email, read newsgroups, and pick up contact listings.

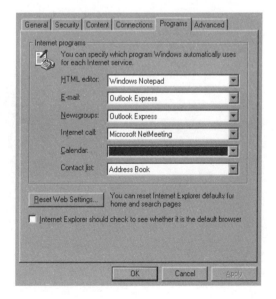

Advanced Tab

From here you can enable/disable a wide range of the advanced IE settings. For most operations, the default settings will be sufficient. However, you might like to experiment with the more obvious settings to improve the overall performance. An example might be to

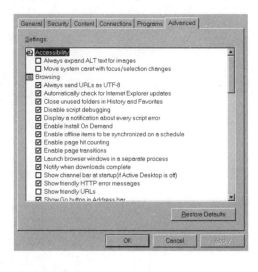

disable some of the Multimedia functions so that certain pages load faster. Use the 'Restore Defaults' to reset the default settings.

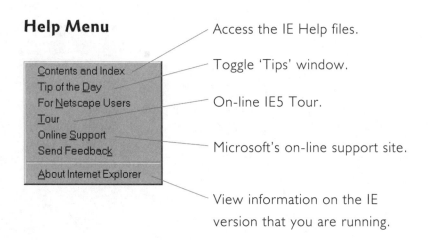

For more detailed coverage of Internet Explorer get the book on it within this same series.

Help Menu

Access the IE Help files.

Toggle 'Tips' window.

On-line IE5 Tour.

Microsoft's on-line support site.

View information on the IE version that you are running.

The World Wide Web

The World Wide Web is a rather grand term used to describe the sum total of all of the web pages available over the Internet. It is more commonly described simply as 'the web'.

The size and scope of 'the web' is near impossible to describe accurately. Not only does it cover most of the nations on earth, it also necessarily covers most of the languages on earth. The number of 'links' between all of these pages is equally vast. Added to this is the fact that web pages are currently being designed and added to this total at an ever increasing rate.

The result of all of this is that finding your way around, or navigating, the web can be difficult, especially for the beginner.

To browse the web you simply need access to the Internet and a 'Web Browser' software package loaded onto your PC.

The URL

The process of browsing the web is a matter of using 'Uniform Resource Locators' or URLs. Every web page on the Internet has an address in the form of a URL. A 'Web Site' is simply a collection of web pages, and usually a web site will have a Home Page which will serve as the starting point for navigating around the rest of the web site. Thus you need to know the URL of the web site home page in order to make best use of the site. It is perfectly possible to gain access to any part of a web site if you happen to know the URL for a particular page, but in general terms you will find that 'beginning at the beginning' of a web site is the best way of navigating around a particular site.

A 'URL' is more commonly known as a 'web site address' and will often take the form;

'http://www.name.type.location'

with each part of the URL being separated by a full stop or the spoken 'dot'.

The 'http://' part of the URL is a command to indicate that the communication process involves '**h**ypertext **t**ransfer **p**rotocol'. On many browsers, it is not necessary to include this as the browser will assume that 'http' is being used.

Other similar commands that you may come across include 'ftp://' which will create a 'file transfer protocol' connection for transferring files, and 'telnet://' which will create a 'telnet' session allowing a kind of screen and keyboard control of a remote computer.

The 'www' part of the URL simply indicates that the required resource is a web site, and is nearly always needed.

The rest of the URL is the addressing part.

The 'name' part is simply that: a name that is given to the web site. The 'type' part will normally indicate the type of web site – 'co' for company, 'org' for organisation, or 'gov' for government department.

New types of URLs will shortly become available, using such names as '.info' for information sites, and '.shop' for on-line shopping.

The 'location' part of the URL indicates the country that the web site is derived from – 'uk' for United Kingdom or 'au' for Australia.

Shorter forms of the URL are also used, most commonly the 'www.companyname.com' form for large companies, and the 'www.name.net' form for what is known as a 'virtual domain'.

Very shortly the range of available URLs will be increased dramatically with the addition of new 'types' – 'store' for electronic retail, and 'info' for information services.

So how do you know where to go? Where do these URLs come from?

Like finding out someone's telephone number, they either tell you themselves, or you need to search some kind of reference resource like a phone book. Finding a web page is a similar process; you will either be given the URL by way of some form of marketing, or by reference to a global URL search resource.

The Search Engine

Finding the information that you need on the World Wide Web is a skill that needs some practice. There are many different types of 'Search Engine' now available that can help with this process.

A Search Engine is basically a highly sophisticated set of web pages that allow you to enter a set of 'key words' relevant to the information that you are looking for. The various search engines are usually informed of the location of new web sites by their developers. The 'Engine' then automatically visits the web site, collects certain elements within the content of the site, and then intelligently stores this information in a database.

Once the key words are entered, the search engine then searches through its database of known web sites for a match between the key words that you have entered and the information contained in the database. It then dynamically produces a new web page which lists the results of the search as a series of new URL links which you can then follow to take you to the information that you are looking for.

These results are frequently graded according to the number of database 'hits' that have been made, presenting the highest number of hits at the top of the returned list. This then gives you a way of judging which of the listed sites are most likely to contain the information that you are looking for.

The skill comes in knowing what 'key words' to enter into the search engine to produce the kind of results that you want. Different key words will produce different results.

The World Wide Web...cont'd

 Many search engines allow sophisticated search methods that use 'Boolean' codes. Check the search engine 'help files' to use these facilities.

Although the search engines are very sophisticated, they are not yet truly 'intelligent' (yet!), and so they do not inherently 'understand' what you may be looking for.

So, as an example, a search for 'York' will produce thousands of results about 'New York', as there will be many more web site entries concerning the latter.

As there is no standard for search engine design, different search engines work in slightly different ways, so the same keywords will also give different results when entered into different search engines.

The popular search engines are those that are truly global – that is, they attempt to collect information on all sites everywhere, regardless of content. This type of search engine has its disadvantages, as the search for 'York' example shows.

Most of the global search engines do attempt to categorise the vast array of web sites according to content, allowing you to search specific areas, but this approach will always be less than perfect.

This problem has given rise to a range of specialised search engines which, for example, restrict themselves to a specific country. This type of specialisation will inevitably continue to the extent where it will not be very long before you are able to search a local search engine that deals only with web content specific to your town, very much like the local phone directory.

An example of a typical search engine search follows:

Search Engine – Example Search

To illustrate a typical search, lets take the example of the search for 'York'. Imagine you are a tourist hoping to visit the historical City of York in the UK, and are looking for information on accommodation and tourist attractions.

I've used one of the longest established global search engines, the 'Web Crawler' search engine.

Firstly, in order to initially restrict our search, we click on the relevant web site category from the list of categories on the Web Crawler Homepage (not shown) – ie, the Travel section. This produces the following web page.

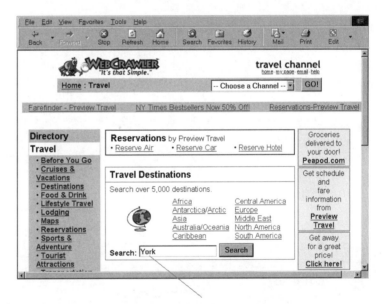

We then enter the key word 'York' into the search input box, and follow the 'Take Me There' link button. The Web Crawler database section concerning travel destinations is then searched using this key word.

The search results are then dynamically compiled into a list and the resulting web page is displayed as follows:

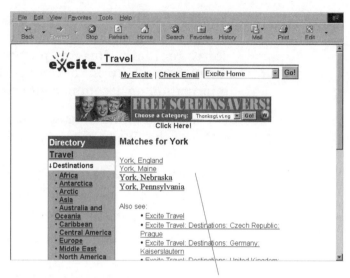

As expected, this search has found many 'hits' for web pages aimed at the New York tourist. However, the search engine has supplied other possible links containing the 'York' key word, one of which is the one that we are seeking. Clicking on this link displays the following.

See the inside back cover of this book for a list of Internet titles within the "in easy steps" series.

Our search has been successful and we can now browse the various sites concerning 'York, England – tourist information'.

E-mail – Outlook Express

Included as part of the Windows 98 package is the Outlook Express program. This program contains several functions including an E-mail package, a Newsgroup reader, and a Directory Services facility. You may recall from the previous discussion that newsgroups are essentially a specialised kind of e-mail system, and consequently the setup procedures are very similar for both. You will find that the Directory Service comes pre-configured for several of the most popular directory look-up sites.

We will look at configuring the e-mail/newsgroup features, after first making sure that Outlook Express is installed.

Installing Outlook Express

When Windows 98 was installed for the first time, the option to install Outlook Express was presented as an option, so it may already be installed. If not, then proceed as follows:

1 Click on 'Start > Settings > Control Panel > Add/Remove Programs'.

2 Select the 'Windows Setup' tab from the 'Add/Remove Programs Properties' window.

3 Select 'Microsoft Outlook Express' from the list of available options (scroll down).

4 Click on 'OK'. You will then be instructed to insert the Windows 98 CD-ROM, if it is not already in place.

Configuring for E-mail

When you sign up with an ISP you will usually be offered an e-mail service, and the ISP will provide you with the necessary configuration and password details to allow you to use this. This information should include the following:

- Your e-mail address.

- Your User or Host name.

- The name or IP address of the Mail Server.

- Your user Password.

Once you have this information, proceed as follows:

1 Start the Outlook Express program, either by double-clicking on the Outlook Express icon on the desktop, or by clicking on 'Start > Programs > Internet Explorer > Outlook Express'.

2 Click on 'Tools' in the menu bar, and select 'Accounts'.

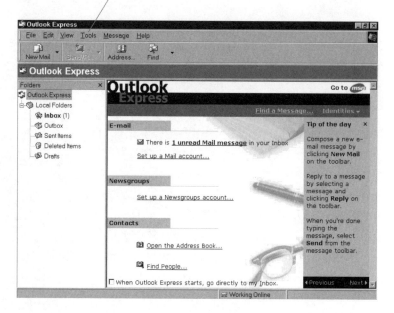

...cont'd

3 Select the 'Mail' tab from the Internet Accounts window.

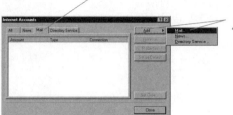

4 Click on 'Add' and then select the 'Mail' option. This will start the 'Internet Connection Wizard'.

5 Enter your name into the 'Display name' entry dialogue box, and click on 'Next>'.

6 Enter your E-mail address as assigned by your ISP, and click 'Next>'.

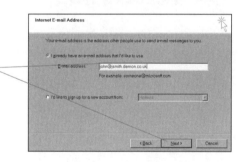

7 Enter the address of the 'incoming' and 'outgoing' Mail Servers as supplied by your ISP. Alternatively, enter the IP addresses. The example shows these for a Demon account, but for other ISPs the incoming and outgoing address may be the same. Click on 'Next'.

8 Enter your e-mail 'User' or 'Host' name as supplied by your ISP, and your e-mail 'Password'. Click on 'Next>'

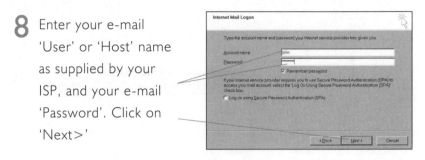

9 Click on Finish.

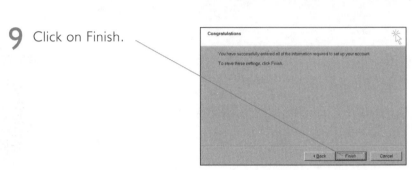

For a more comprehensive look at Outlook Express and it's big brother Microsoft Outlook, you should refer to *Outlook 2000 in easy steps*. Please see the inside back cover for a list of titles within this series and check the company website for availability and any other new titles.

The E-mail account profile that you have just created (you may have named it differently) will now appear in the Mail - Accounts window, and you are ready to collect and send your e-mails. If you wish you can first check these settings by selecting the profile and then clicking on the 'Properties' button, where you can change any of the settings if required. To return to the main program, click on 'Close'.

Using E-mail

To send an e-mail, proceed as follows:

1   Click on the 'Compose Message' icon in the toolbar at the top left hand corner of the main program window.

2   In the 'New Mail' window, enter the e-mail address of the recipient at the cursor, which should be open next to 'To:'. This could be your own e-mail address if you wish.

3   Click in the empty message window below this, and type in your message.

4   Click on 'Send' at the top left hand corner. This will place your message in the 'Outbox', which is a temporary storage area for messages waiting to be delivered.

5   Click on the 'Send and Receive' icon in the main toolbar. Outlook Express will then attempt to open a connection to your ISP. If you are prompted for a username and password, simply click on 'OK' without attempting to change the details.

Your e-mail will now be sent to your ISP's mail server, from which it will be passed onto the recipient's mail server and thus on to the recipient. At the same time, any mail that has been sent to you will be automatically downloaded into your 'Inbox'. You do not need to be sending mail in order to receive it however. Simply click on 'Send and Receive' at any time to download any messages that are being sent to you.

Configuring for Newsgroups

As previously mentioned, setting up for newsgroups is very similar to setting up for e-mail. You will need to know the address of your ISP's news server.

1 From the main Outlook Express window, click on 'Tools > Accounts' and then select the 'News' tab.

2 Click on 'Add' and select the 'News' option.

3 Click through the 'Name' and 'E-mail address' sections by clicking on 'Next>', as both should automatically pick up your existing settings.

4 Enter the address of your ISP's news server, and continue by clicking 'Next>'.

5 Click on Finish.

The newly created Newsgroup profile will be displayed in the Accounts window, and once again you can check these settings by selecting the profile and clicking on 'Properties'.

When you click on 'Close' you will be asked if you wish to download the list of available Newsgroups from the newsgroup server. You will need to do this at some stage anyway if you wish to use the Newsgroups, but be warned: at the time of writing there were approximately 31,000 newsgroups available, and downloading them all may take some time. You might decide to delay this process until a suitable off-peak time.

...cont'd

When using Newsgroups, make sure you are familiar with 'Netiquette' – that is, the do's and don'ts of communicating with your fellow cyber surfers. For more information on this, see Internet Culture, also in the 'in easy steps' series.

Using Newsgroups

Once you have downloaded the list of newsgroups from the newsgroup server, you will be able to participate by viewing messages, posting replies, or by posting your own questions. First, however, you will need to find the newsgroups that cover your area(s) of interest, and then subscribe to them.

Suppose that your interest is in 'fishing'. Find the newsgroups that cover this area of interest as follows:

1 Select the newsgroup server entry from the Outlook Express listing in the left hand window, and answer 'Yes' to the question 'Would you like to view a list of available newsgroups?'.

2 Enter the word 'fishing' into the 'Display newsgroups' dialogue.

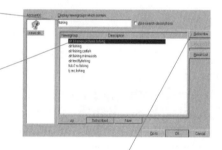

3 From the resulting list, select the newsgroup you wish to subscribe to.

4 Click on the 'Subscribe' button (you can subscribe to several at a time), and then click on 'OK'.

5 The newsgroup(s) that you have subscribed to will then appear in the main program window. Click on one of them to download the current list of message headings in that newsgroup.

6 Clicking on any message heading will then download that particular message in the message display window. You can then use the icons in the main toolbar to reply to that message or to post your question.

FTP and Archie

One of the most common uses of the Internet is to find and download files from remote sites.

File Transfer Protocol
One of the best ways of downloading files is via an Internet protocol known as FTP, short for 'file transfer protocol'.

For an FTP link to function, the remote 'ftp server' computer must be running a specialised FTP program, your local PC must be running an FTP 'client' program, and there must be a live IP link or 'session' running between them. Under most circumstances, an FTP transfer is usually done using one of two methods.

The most frequent method involves downloading files from web sites using a web browser. More often that not this process is invisible to the user, as most of the popular web browsers now incorporate an FTP client. The embedded FTP client starts automatically when it encounters an 'ftp' indentifier at the beginning of a URL link within a web page, and the file transfer proceeds until completed when the FTP client automatically shuts down.

 Many files available over the Internet are compressed into 'zip' files, and need to be decompressed before they can be used. The 'Winzip' utility is one of the more popular applications to do this, and this can also be found on the Internet.

Another method is to use an FTP client application running independently of a web browser. We will now look at using one of the most popular FTP applications, the WS_FTP program. The 'Limited Edition' is available without charge to non-commercial users, and can be located and downloaded over the Internet using a search engine as described earlier.

WS_FTP Limited Edition
Written by John A Junod, this application is one of the best examples of freely available Internet software. It can be used to view files on a remote FTP server, and then download them to your local hard disk as required.

Once you have obtained a copy, unzipped it, and have it installed, it will look something like the following when you start it up.

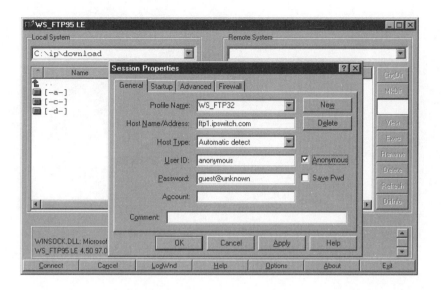

This interface allows you to use a number of predefined ftp 'session' settings known as session 'profiles'. Each session profile refers to a different ftp server, which can be located anywhere in the world. The profile shown happens to point to the source of the WS_FTP program (ie, an ftp server with the domain name 'ftp1.ipswitch.com'). The details of these settings are as follows:

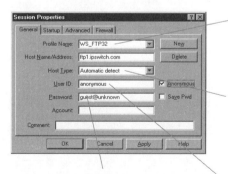

The profile name

There are many different types of ftp servers or 'hosts': the 'Automatic detect' setting however will be suitable for most sessions

The accepted password for the 'anonymous' login is your e-mail address, or the above spoof e-mail address.

Most publicly available ftp servers use 'anonymous' as the login name; other more restricted servers will require a known login name

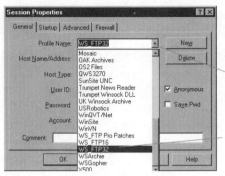

If you click on the drop-down button for the 'Profile Name' entry, you will see a list of the predefined ftp sessions, with the current 'WS_FTP' server highlighted

To see this application in action you will need first to be connected to the Internet. Once you are 'on-line', click on 'OK' within the 'Session Properties' window. This will start the 'WS_FTP' session.

The 'Session Properties' window will disappear, leaving the main program window.

You will notice a series of instructions and replies scroll past in the lower left hand corner of this window as the session is established with the remote server. Once this is completed you will see the following:

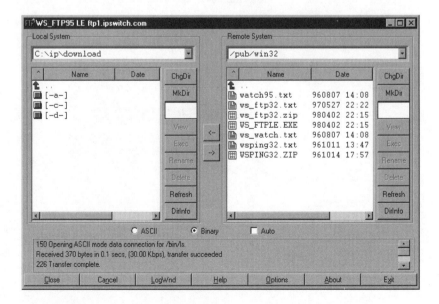

This view is simply a directory listing of files on the local and remote systems.

In the left hand window you will see your local hard drive (which on my system I had previously set to a directory with the path C:\ip\download), and in the right hand window you will see a view of the available files on the remote server at 'ftp1.ispwitch.com/pub/win32'. This includes the directory 'pub', which is normally where the publicly available files are stored.

When you click on 'Close' the current ftp session will be closed down. When this has been successful, the 'Close' button will change to the 'Connect' button.

We will now attempt to download a file that we will be able to use later.

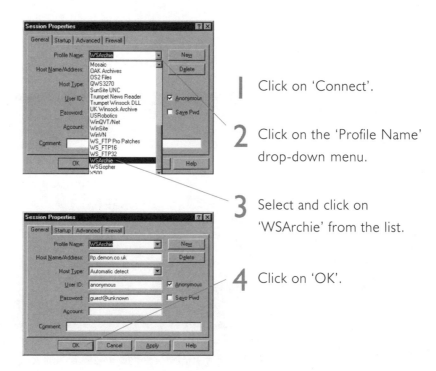

1 Click on 'Connect'.

2 Click on the 'Profile Name' drop-down menu.

3 Select and click on 'WSArchie' from the list.

4 Click on 'OK'.

Once the session is established, you will see the following:

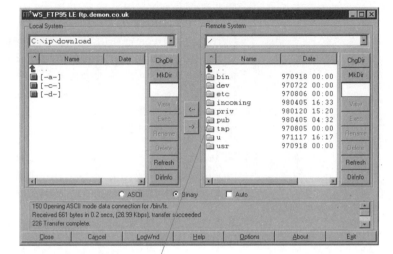

Double-clicking on a directory folder icon will display the files and sub-directories within that directory.

5 Double-click on the 'pub' directory listing, and then keep clicking on the path '/pub/ibmpc/win95/winsock/apps/ wsarchie', until you reach the 'wsarchie' directory as follows:

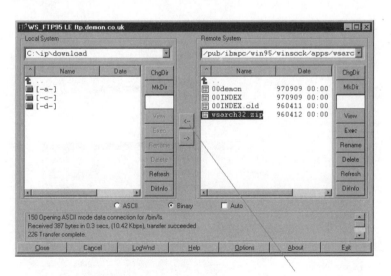

6 Select the file 'wsarch32.zip' and click on the '<--' button. This will begin the file transfer.

7 During the file transfer process you will see the following window, indicating the progress of the transfer.

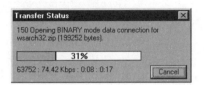

8 On completion, the file will appear in the local directory together with a 'log' file. This file is a text record of the transaction.

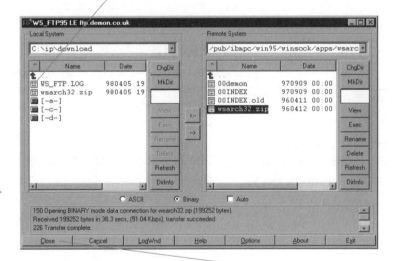

Don't forget to disconnect from the Internet once you have finished with it.

9 Shut down the ftp session by clicking on 'Close'.

The wsarch32.zip file can now be unzipped and installed in a new directory, ready for the next section.

Archie

Downloading files using the FTP protocol is fine if you know where the files are located. If you do not, then WSArchie (written by David Woaked) is a handy utility that can find files for you, provided you have a rough idea of what the filename is. Archie is mostly a server that maintains an up-to-date database of all of the known files that are available for ftp downloading. You can then access this database via an Archie client, which allows you to supply the filename that you are looking for, and then monitor the search process. A list of all known locations for that file is then supplied via the client. You can then setup the Archie client so that when you click on any of the results, the FTP client is automatically started, and the file is downloaded to your local disk.

WSARCHIE

Use Winzip or any other suitable file decompression utility to unzip files.

Assuming that you have successfully downloaded, unzipped, and installed the 'wsarch32.zip' file that we located in the previous section, we can setup WSArchie as follows:

1. Without connecting to the Internet, run the WSArchie program.

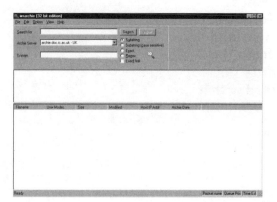

2. Click on 'Option' in the toolbar, and then click on 'Ftp Setup'.

...cont'd

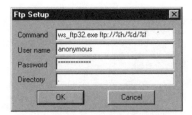

3 The ftp settings are largely pre-entered as shown.

Create an easily located sub-directory called 'download' to receive incoming files.

4 If you are using the WS_FTP95 program you will need to adjust the command line setting to suit, as well as to add the appropriate path.

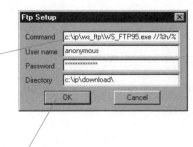

5 You can also add a suitable 'Directory' path. This is where the downloaded files will be placed. When completed, click on 'OK'.

You can now use the WSArchie program as follows:

1 Connect to the Internet, and then run WSARCHIE.

Connect to the Internet by clicking on the short-cut to the ISP connection profile that you created in the Start menu.

2 Enter the name of the file you are looking for into 'Search for'. As an example we will search for a popular e-mail package, Eudora Lite, with the file name 'eul305.exe'

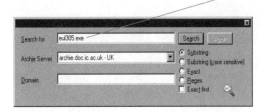

3 If you are searching from outside the UK, click on the 'Archie Server' drop-down menu and then select and click on your nearest server.

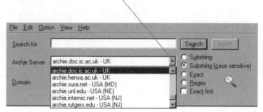

4 Click on 'Search'. After a short while Archie will produce a set of search results as follows:

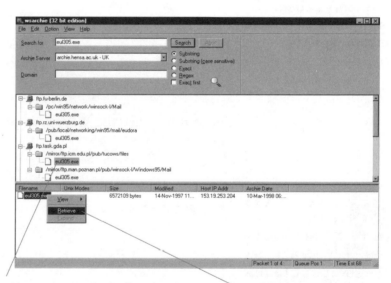

If you are using a modem to connect to the Internet, don't forget to disconnect after the Archie session is completed.

5 Click on any of the file entries so that it appears in the lower window, then right-click on this entry.

6 Click on 'Retrieve'.

The file should now download automatically into the directory specified, using the FTP program.

Useful Names and Addresses

Cabling (etc), Conduits & Backboxes

CITY ELECTRICAL FACTORS –
495 UK branches

1 Station Road
Kenilworth
Warwickshire CV8 1JJ

Tel: +44 (0)1926 858127
+44 (0)1926 851467

Tools, Faceplates, & Connectors

CABLELINES

Unit 4
Orchard Business Park
Sandiacre
Nottingham NG10 5BP
(Cat 5 UTP Jacks will be different from those specified in the text)

Tel: +44 (0)115 949 1010

WADSWORTH

London:
Birmingham:
Bristol:
Warrington:
Cumbernauld:
Website:

Tel: +44 (0)181 268 7006
Tel: +44 (0)121 697 1000
Tel: +44 (0)145 489 2700
Tel: +44 (0)192 566 3600
Tel: +44 (0)141 300 4000
http://www.wadsworth.co.uk

MAPLIN –
42 UK branches

Nearest branch (UK):
To order a catalogue:
Website:

Tel: 0800 136156
Tel: +44 (0)1702 554000
https://catalogue.maplin.co.uk

Networking Hardware

3COM

220 Wharfedale Road
Winnersh
Wokingham RG41 5TP

Tel: +44 (0)1189 278200

Demon Internet

Gateway House
322 Regents Park Road
Finchley
London N3 2QQ

Tel: +44 (0)181 371 1234

Part Numbers

	Cablelines	Wadsworth	Maplin
WALL BOX			
Coax – 44mm	BB6	280-7050	
Twisted Pair			
– 37mm		280-7105	
– 32mm	BB2		
COAX			
RG 58 Cable	2907	9907	XS51F
BNC Connector	B35A41JB	350-1010	DN99H
Strain Relief Boot	10872998	350-9000	CK08J
T Piece Adapter	B35P31J9	350-3200	DP08J
50 Ohm Terminator	B35Z98J5	350-5000	CK06G
Faceplate (inc Barrels)	001065	281-4020	CD55K & DV21X
Crimp Tool	1302 & 2075	290-2105 & 290-2106	PZ19V
Cable Stripper	Cable Stripper	290-3170	JH18U
Patch Cable – 2m	BNC2M	090-4002	TV81C
Cable Tester	RCSniffer	720-2020	CU68Y
TWISTED PAIR			
Cat 5 UTP Cable	900004	062-8132	VB20W
RJ45 UTP Plug	5554720	610-1085	JT49D
Strain Relief Boot	8850062	610-1035	CG00A
Cat 5 UTP Jack (258A/EIA 568B)	BO11A0012	610-1386	CG25C
Faceplate			
– single		280-0080	
– double	011102	280-0085	
Crimp Tool	1302 & 2064	290-3522	PZ18U
Insertion Tool	0400001	600-1455	
Patch Cable – 2m	Patch 2m	092-1020	CD34M
Cable Tester	RCSniffer	720-2037	CU66W
ETHERNET HUB	ADHUB8CT	726-3201	VL93B

Index